# THE WAY

SPIRIT FROM THE WELL

Also by Philip Rose

The Rose Studio

*A primer of Celestial Navigation*, 2006

*Tao Te King*, 2006

*Last Letter from a Father to his Son*, 2007; *A Small Book of Symbols*, 2007

*A Book of Sonnets*, 2007; *Sonnets of Love*, 2007

*Reflections on Sacrifice*, 2008;

*Some Random Jottings on Astrology & the Zodiac*, 2008

*Some Musings on Jesus Christ*, 2009

*What is Enlightenment*, 2009; *More thoughts on Enlightenment*, 2009

*The Sea & what it means to me*, 2009

*More Random Jottings on Astrology & the Zodiac*, 2009

*Reincarnation*, 2010

*The Pilgrim*, 2011; *Janus*, 2011; *Advaita*, 2011

*Some Ponderings on the Possible Significance of 2012*, 2011

*Love*, 2012; *Mythos & Logos*, 2012

*The Young Man & The Old Man. A Dialogue*, 2012

*The Ten Bulls of Kakuan*, 2013; *Pebbles on the Beach*, 2013

*What is the Holy Grail?*, 2014; *Thoughts on Freedom*, 2014

*Some Small Sea Sketches*, 2014

*Being*, 2014; *The Problem of Evil*, 2014

*Tao Te King* (2nd Edition), 2014

*Waves of the Sea*, 2015; *Paradox*, 2015

*Where the River Bends*, 2015

*A Way of Life*, 2016

*The Way*, 2017

Novels

*The Atlan Roll*, 2008

*The Beam*, 2009

*Beyond the Beam*, 2010

Chippenham Picton Publishing

Tales of Old Wal, stories for Children 1975

The Halliday Review

Selected Poems

# THE WAY

## SPIRIT FROM THE WELL

A way of life for the modern world
based on the teachings of the ancient wisdom

by
Philip Rose

Melchisedec Press

# Melchisedec Press

5 Taylor Road, Altrincham, Cheshire WA14 4LR
melchisedecpress.net
info@melchisedecpress.net
philoldford5@gmail.com

Published in the UK in 2019 by Melchisedec Press

Edited by Hephzibah Yohannan

The rights of Philip Rose have been asserted by him in accordance with Copyright Designs and Patents Act.

The moral right of the author is asserted.

Text, Haiku with Frontispiece, Poems on pages 9, 32-34, 55, 98, 101-130
© Philip Rose & Hephzibah Yohannan

Cover, Frontispiece and interior Illustrations & cover design
© Philip Rose & Hephzibah Yohannan

The book titles were previously published individually by The Rose Studio

All rights reserved. No part of this publication may be reproduced, stored in a retrieval system or transmitted in any form or by any means without the prior permission in writing of the publisher, nor be otherwise circulated in any form of binding or cover other than that in which it is published without a similar condition, including this condition, being imposed on the subsequent purchaser.

ISBN 978-1-872240-42-8 (hardback)
ISBN 978-1-872240-43-5 (paperback)

A CIP catalogue record for this book is available from the British Library

Printed and bound by Ingram Spark
Set in Baskerville

Sea sky ——————— sky sea,
Merging, separating, merging,
A lone vessel.

## Dedication

For my dear departed wife Elizabeth with whom I shared sixty-seven years of loving companionship. As Thea Rose she is the author of *Mindshift: With Eyes Half Closed*

# Contents

| | | |
|---|---|---|
| Introduction | | i |
| Book 1: The Way | | 1 |
|     Foreword | | 2 |
|     Part One | The Origin | 4 |
|     Part Two | The Coming To Be | 12 |
|     Part Three | Being. The Return | 23 |
| Book 2: What is Enlightenment? | | 35 |
| Book 3: More Thoughts on Enlightenment | | 44 |
| Book 4: Paradox | | 55 |
| Book 5: Janus | | 64 |
| Book 6: Being | | 70 |
| Book 7: A Way of Life | | 82 |
| Book 8: Sonnets of Love | | 99 |

# Introduction

This book brings together a collection of short books published over a number of years by Philip Rose. They detail his lifelong search for the meaning of life, his meeting with his friend and mentor Eugene Halliday, and his deep spiritual experiences when alone at sea. An actor, artist, writer, and family man, Philip is also a solo trans-Atlantic yachtsman.

Now aged 94, Philip is still writing to express and share his spiritual philosophy drawn from many years of study and meditation. His expression, in simple language, of his experiences, at the same time both human and transcendent, conveys the heart of that state of being, described and taught in the most precise language by Eugene Halliday, in his book *Reflexive Self-Consciousness*.

This book ends with a series of Sonnets which, in the spirit of the Sufi poets, expresses through the experience and language of human love, the highest love of the Divine, the true Self of selves.

Hephzibah Yohannan 2019

This collection of my books has been brought together and published here by the Melchisedec Press, which was founded by David Mahlowe to publish the work of Eugene Halliday. The Melchisedec Press is now edited by Hephzibah Yohannan, Eugene Halliday's literary and artistic executor, with whom I hereby share the copyright of my work.

Philip Rose 2019

# Book 1

# THE WAY

## SPIRIT FROM THE WELL

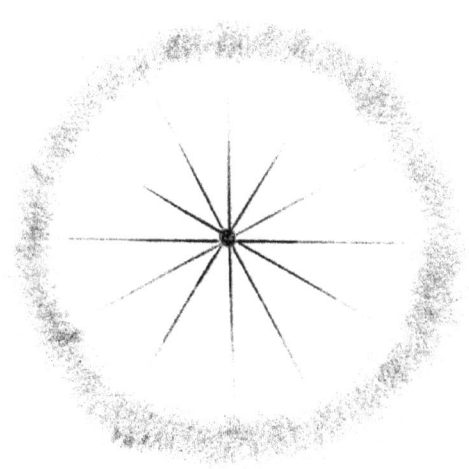

A Way of Life for the modern world based
on the teachings of the Ancient Wisdom.

I AM THE WAY, THE TRUTH AND THE LIFE

JOHN 14:6

## Foreword

I began this little book in my 91$^{st}$ year. It tells of what I have come to believe after a lifetime of seeking for what is the meaning of life and how one should live that life at its optimum level. I cannot prove it for it is ultimately not susceptible to the usual scientific methods of proof for it all lies in a different realm of reality although its main tenets are behind the main religions of the world and go back to mankind's earliest thinkings and feelings. Believe it or not, as you will. All I can say it has sustained me throughout my life and made that life harmonious and joyous.

The teachings of which I speak are often referred to as the Ancient Wisdom. I first came across them at the age of 25 when I met a very wise man, although I don't think I ever heard him refer to them as such. The phrase he used to describe the ultimate result of his teaching was Reflexive Self Consciousness, which I subsequently came to realise was the same as that of the Ancient Wisdom. His teaching was the same as that taught by those of old, though expressed in more modern terms. His name was Eugene Halliday. He died in 1987 and is comparatively unknown, although he has been described as one of the great spirits of the modern age; a website exists – just click on his name – which gives masses of information and allows most of his writings to be downloaded for free. He once said 'My day will come'. I know it will and it has been the greatest privilege of my life to have known Eugene and to know that I owe my life to him.

I am no academic or scholar or learned man. (It is written that an academic is an ass with a load of books on his back.) I am merely an old and simple humble man who writes for the average 'man in the street' who has no time left to think on these things but may like to know more. I think of him –for I am one –as someone who has been brought up as a Western European Christian. For this reason, for clarity, I often use the word God when it's more accurate to use the word Godhead in referring to the Infinite Power. God is secondary, being already a formed entity, and the being usually worshipped by Christians. Keep this in mind.

In the Afterword to Part One I say 'All I have written so far is simply a multitude of words. They no more explain the meaning of God or of Life or of the origin of things than pie in the sky for it is all unexplainable and far beyond the power of words. Do you know what Life is. No. Yet you know that you are alive, that is all you need to know. Then why do I write. Lao Tzu, the great Chinese mystic, wrote:

> Those who speak do not know
> Those who know do not speak

Yet when he left the city to live in solitude in the mountains the gatekeeper asked him to write down his wisdom for the benefit of his fellow men, so he stayed the night and produced the great classic of the Tao Te Ching.

In the story of the scorpion and the frog, a scorpion wished to cross a river so he asked a kindly frog to take him across. 'No' said the frog 'You will sting me'. 'I promise not to' replied the scorpion. So the frog reluctantly took him on his back and began to swim across. Halfway over the frog felt a jab 'Now what have you done. We'll both drown'. 'I'm very sorry' said the scorpion – I couldn't help it, it's just my nature'.

I write because it is 'just my nature'

Philip Rose

## Part One. The Origin.

### *ALL IS ONE*

This refers to there being but one power that is the origin of all there is. Apart from this power there is nothing. This power is in and behind all phenomena. It is formless and yet causes all forms to come into existence. Above all it is sentient, that is it feels and knows itself, it is not blind and purposeless.

To understand something we give it a name hence this power has many names, as God and Godhead, Allah, Brahman, Tao, Absolute and Absolute Sentient Power, First Cause, Primum Mobile and so on. Yet this power is beyond all naming. These names mean nothing. It can never be described in words. Yet it is the origin of everything. What it is in essence can only be felt, be experienced. Its essence cannot be understood intellectually. It has been — and can be today — experienced, almost, in its fullness by some of those we call mystics throughout the ages. Yet most people at some point in their lives have had a dim glimpse of this Power, have felt a stirring of wonder and awe at the mystery at the heart of things. We all come from this power and for the most part we are ignorant partakers of this power. The purpose of life is for the being to pass beyond its sense of separateness and realise and then regain its union with this power. The return to its true and real home. Jacob Boehme calls the Infinite Power 'The Ungrund'. It is a sentient void, nothingness, that is no thing, yet it is the source of all things. It is Absolute Freedom.

---

### *ALL IS TWO*

This refers to the twofold aspect of existence. Everything is bi-fold. To define something its opposite is implied.: Good requires Evil, True requires False, Beauty requires Ugly. This twofold aspect of Life originated necessarily in the First Cause, the Initial Power. Before the beginning this power was alone, there was nothing except it. It has no beginning, it will have no end, it is infinite and eternal. It can never die, it can never cease to be. It feels its aloneness (all oneness), which is to us, and possibly is also to the Infinite Power, a terrible thing. How it actually feels to itself, the human heart and mind can never fully comprehend. Imagine being the only person alive in the whole world. For ever. At a certain point it decides to do something: it decides to create. It does this because that is its nature. Possibly also because it is something to do to alleviate its aloneness. It decides to discover itself, find out what it can do. For it can do anything for there is no one else to stop it. It can be considered as playing a game with itself, a game that gives it the utmost joy. It decides to manifest, to bring out into the open what is inside itself, hidden in potentia. It decides to produce forms from the formless. Many myths tell the story of a god who sees a beautiful damsel and pursues her. Each time he catches up with her she changes shape and runs away again. Thus are born all the various forms and shapes of the universe. So it divides itself from itself. The formless gives birth to the formed The latter is the universe. How it does this, I try to inadequately describe in a subsequent section. Behind, and yet in, the universe remains the formless. This twofold aspect, the formless and the formed is a reality, yet also at the same time an illusion. The universe is the shadow of the real, and the only real is the formless, the sentient God. From a certain viewpoint the Good, the True and the Beautiful are the formless; the Evil, False and Ugly are the formed. The former we call God, the latter the universe. These two are one but also not two (see next section). The universe can be said to be the body of God, while the Good, True and Beautiful is his consciousness. Just as you have a body which is formed and visible and a consciousness which is formless and invisible, so with God. You and God are one and the same though on vastly different scales and seen from reverse viewpoints: God moves down into form, Man moves upward to the formless.

---

### *ALL IS NOT ONE, NOT TWO.*

This is a difficult idea to understand. A certain leap of the imagination is required, (The Indian Sanscrit word is *Advaita* meaning precisely this. and a whole Vedanta philosophy of non-duality has been built on the concept.) Put another way, everything is nothing yet everything is something. It has been said that God is an infinite sphere whose centre is everywhere and whose circumference is nowhere, (I can understand if you are now completely bewildered. It all sounds so impossible, a paradox of paradoxes but bear with me.) We live always in this situation but do not realise it. The purpose of life is simply to realise it. This we do by clearing away all concepts of separativity. (How we do this I do my best to explain in Part Two.)

Eugene Halliday called the state of non duality when reached, Reflexive Self Consciousness which is a state of transcendental consciousness which he said that if humanity realised its huge importance their whole effort would be directed to achieving it. Furthermore he said that the ultimate survival of mankind depended on their so doing.

What does it mean to say everything is nothing yet everything is something. We live in a world of opposites, a world where things are either/or. 'You can't have your cake and eat it', as the saying goes. 'Make up your mind, it's one thing or the other.' This is the function of the rational mind which operates solely by comparing one thing with another. The rational mind is not creative, it simply compares and evaluates one thing or idea in order to reach a conclusion or find which is fit for purpose. But there is another way, a higher mind which rises above these two contrasting things or ideas by bringing them together into a new emergent. This is *Advaita,* not one not two, or non duality. The original *Advaita* is the creation process itself, for this is the formless limiting itself in order to create form from itself while still remaining formless itself. (How it does this is described in the last section.) The first emergent has arisen. The only image I can think of to give a glimpse of this apparently contradictory and impossible state of affairs is to think in terms of yourself, for you are a body which is overseen by your sense of awareness of yourself. The body is visible to the senses while the overseeing is invisible. (It is no good saying the awareness is simply a product of the function of the visible brain for this has not as yet been proven and probably never will be. It is equally permissible to say the brain itself has been produced by the awareness, i.e. consciousness, in order to provide for itself a vehicle by which to manifest itself. This is the understanding of all the best ancient authorities and mystics.) The formless causes the formed as a vehicle for its own manifestation, just as your own consciousness or awareness is the ultimate cause of your physical existence. (This is heretical to modern scientific thought, though that thought is still trying to determine exactly what consciousness really is.) All ancient teachings, as well as modern theologians, speak of the 'Mind of God'. This mind produces the universe — God said 'Let there be light' and there was light. His word, which is invisible, produced the world.

---

## ALL IS THREE

This refers to the new emergent. In life everything goes by threes. 'Third time lucky.' For anything to come into existence there must be first a force, second there must be a resistance to that force and finally there is the result of the force pressing against what resists it. Press your closed fist against your open palm. Press harder and harder. The result. A slight pain perhaps, but definitely, if the pressure is maintained, warmth, heat. Heat. And heat is the origin of the universe. Resistance causes heat. The universe comes about by heat. This is why resistance is necessary to life. Positive and negative: male and female: good and evil. Both are necessary. Everywhere you look you find the threefold process operating. The most obvious example is when you do anything. First you have a will and feeling you wish to do something or you wish to know and understand something, second you think or plan how to go about it, third you do it. Think of any process you like it's always threefold. In philosophy it is expressed in the terms of Thesis, Antithesis, Synthesis. In psychology it is Conation, Affection, Cognition. It is the Trinity doctrine of the Christian faith, the three triangles of the Sephiroth of the Jewish Qabala. It is the three gods or principles of Hinduism — Brahma, Vishnu and Shiva — and the Trikaya system of the three bodies of the Buddha. In ancient Egypt it is Osiris, Isis and Horus. Finally, the Chinese of the Tao, the Tao-Te-Ching and the I Ching is full everywhere of threeness with the Yin Yang and the constant interplay of change between the two. Tao stresses the concept of Heaven and Earth with Man as the mediator between the two. Heaven is Yin, the spirit, while Earth is Yang, the substance and form: Man is spirit, soul and body. Only Islam, except for the Sufi tradition, as far as I know, is strictly monotheistic and does not accept any concept of threeness.

---

## IMMANENCE AND TRANSCENDENCE

This refers to the Finite (Immanence) and the Infinite (Transcendence). The idea that the Infinite Power is in the formed individual and at the same time in the formless.

Infinite Power. (Remember this Infinite Power is sentient and aware of itself. Sentience is a feeling–knowing state, a more generalised sensation than consciousness which is a more focussed awareness.) This Infinite Power is not the blind force of materialistic science, rather a sensitive intelligent power seeking always to evolve. The power evolves through the workings of the universe it has created, striving always for more and more perfection. (However this power is not merely the somewhat impersonal and abstract force it sounds from how I have described it so far. It is that, but it is also personal and loving. Christ talks if it as Him and My Father. He says 'I and my Father are One. My Father works and I work'. This illustrates well the idea of immanence and transcendence, Christ being immanent in the transcendence that is God. In the same way the Christ in you is immanent in the transcendence.) But there is a paradox here. The Power – or let us now call it also the Father – although it strives ever for more and more perfection, of itself it does not strive for it is already perfect. It is Absolute Being and static; the universe is Becoming and dynamic. Being and Becoming, those are the two states of the One, God, the Father, the source of all there is. The purpose of life is to move from Becoming to Being. The immanence in the depths of the individual is identical with the transcendence of the Infinite Power, God the Father, but writ small. When the individual fully knows and identifies with this he has reached Unity, the ultimate and optimum state for the human being.

---

## LOVE

This refers to what makes the world go round as the popular song has it. How does Love make the world go round. It is said 'God is Love, Love is God'. This is literally true. God loves himself. He loves himself because there is no one else to love. His loving himself is the developing of himself. My mentor, Eugene Halliday, defines Love as 'work to develop the potentialities of being' That is what God does by loving his creation. He discovers himself by manifesting himself through his creation and then developing it which is done by loving it. As I say in the final couplet of one of my Sonnets of Love (No 23):

> Love loves itself, for it can do no other,
> It loves itself when we love one another.

Whether we know it or not, that is what we do when we love. A gardener loves his garden by working to bring it to perfection. Henry Royce, 1833-1933 the designer of the world famous motor car had a motto, 'Any job, however humble, if rightly done is noble.' That is love at work. There is a very interesting novel by the well known author Nevil Shute, 1899-1960, called 'Round the Bend' in which an aircraft ground engineer becomes a kind of Messiah by showing his fellow workers how to be in some sort noble by doing just that. 'Every time you tighten a nut on a cylinder head you must do it properly and not skimp it otherwise you may cause a plane crash. At the same time you advance your soul's development' A similar message is in Robert Pirsig's 'Zen and the art of motorcycle maintenance'. Art is Love. Science is Love when it is done artistically, that is, using the intuition as well as the rational, or the female as well as the male attributes. Another of my Sonnets (No. 50) has a Line:

> Deny Love not — it may not come again.

Have you ever been in love. If not, I pity you. But love has pain as well as joy, 'exquisite pain' I call it in another of my Sonnets. It is the most giddying mad exhilarating experience you can ever have. You want to kiss everyone you meet, you gladly flout all convention, you laugh and cry with joy and sorrow all at once. life is the most wonderful thing. Shakespeare said 'The lunatic, lover and poet are of imagination all compact'. This feeling of being in love is the nearest thing to the state of Being, often termed Enlightenment or Self Realisation.

---

## *TRANSLATION AND ROTATION*

This refers to the two fold motion of the Absolute Power and the method by which it creates the universe. The ancients symbolised this by using the image of a snake. The translating movement was a snake running free: the rotating motion was the snake with its tail in its mouth. You can also think of it as a straight line continually edging round until it finally reaches its starting point. The initial movement of the Absolute simply travels endlessly through space in all and every direction with no end or goal in sight. When it rotates and crosses itself and forms a circle that is its first manifestation or form which is in fact the beginning of the universe. All these attempts to describe what happens are of course only visual images as what is actually happening cannot be described in words for words are definitions and the Absolute Power or God is beyond definition. For instance, another perhaps more accurate description of the process is to imagine God as motionless. He doesn't move at all for he doesn't need to for he is already everywhere. What we call his rotating motion is simply him shifting his attention from one place or possibility to another, as you do when sitting motionless you move your eyes from one place to another thus giving rise to the appearance of motion. Such a shift produces a vortex and darkens, forming a kind of knot as in a knot in a piece of wood. This is the universe. This first knot then becomes a myriad of smaller knots as in the stars and the galaxies. Finally they become ever smaller and smaller knots which are the plants, animals and humans. And remember everything is a living entity for it all comes from a living intelligent source. The so called translating and rotating motions are both the one source behaving in two modes of action. The mystics and many ancient authorities summed it all up as 'An infinite sphere whose centre is everywhere and whose circumference is nowhere'. This is an excellent way of describing it for it is an apparent impossibility. A mindless paradox. This is why I said in All is not One not Two a certain leap of imagination is required. In fact paradox is at the heart of it all. If you truly understand paradox you are there, you have found the secret. The rational faculty can make no sense of it. The intuitional faculty is needed, what is termed Mythos, not Logos.

All of the previous sections have been described sequentially in order to attempt some sort of explanation of what creation is. But in truth all such accounts are only pointers to the essence of reality. They give some indications of how it came about, not what it *actually* is. For everything described is occurring simultaneously. To mention them in sequence is an abstraction and the rational mind at work. The reality is totally otherwise. The infinite sphere with its centre everywhere and its circumference nowhere is a beating heart pulsating and vibrating with vibrant life and radiating in all directions boundlessly. It is Love in action. This is magic. It cannot be explained by reason alone, it must be felt, be experienced as in vision as a living simultaneous wholeness. It is a wonder mystery only to be understood by the open human heart when it speaks to and submits to the Heart of All.

---

### Afterword to Part One.

All I have written so far is simply a multitude of words which no more explain the meaning of God, or of Life, or of the origin of everything than pie in the sky. For it is all unexplainable. What it all is, what Life is can only be felt, be experienced, not explained. Do you know what life is. Yet you know you are alive. That is all you need to know. You know what it is to feel joy, to feel grief. Words define these things, they don't say what joy or grief actually is. The only way to know joy is to be joyful. St Augustine, in answer to the question 'What is time,' replied 'I know, but when you ask me I don't'. And Alan

Watts wrote 'If you ask me to show you God, I will point to the sun, or a tree, or a worm. But if you say "You mean, then, that God is the sun, the tree, the worm and all other things," I shall have to say that you have missed the point entirely'. So why say anything. Exactly so. Yet human nature being what it is one must say something even though it all amounts to nothing. Nothing, however, is what it does indeed all amount to. I have said several times in this writing the meaning can never be explained only felt, be experienced. Writers from all times have named this experience, as – Reflexive Self Consciousness, Resec (Eugene Halliday) – Self Remembering (Gurdjieff) – The Undivided Mind (Alan Watts) – The Now (Eckhart Tolle) – Transcendent Consciousness, Enlightenment, Self Realisation (numerous authors). It has further been called – Being – The Holy Grail – The Noble Eightfold Path (Buddha) – No Mind, Suchness (Zen Buddhism) – The Tao (Chinese) – Samadhi (Hindu) – Satori (Japanese) – and lastly, The Kingdom of Heaven (Christ). There are many more. This was all commonplace in the ancient world though of course practised by only the few. Today the teaching is almost totally unknown, though there are increasing signs of its re-emergence.

I will try, but necessarily unsuccessfully, to say something about what it feels like to have this experience in Part Three, the experience of Being.

---

### Part Two. The Coming To Be.

If you have followed me so far you will have found, I expect, a somewhat dry, arid and abstract description of what the Ancient Wisdom traditional account of creation is, an account incidentally, at variance with orthodox religion. However, they are not really at variance, simply describing the same or similar events from different viewpoints, the orthodox or exoteric being rational and historical, and the Ancient Wisdom being intuitional and esoteric and not concerned with the temporal. The one is concerned with time and successive events and the other with the eternal and simultaneity, the one with theological explanations and so dull and boring, the other with pure experience and living vibrant life.

In this section we merge the two, erring on the side of the latter.

We now move into the area of you the reader and the warmth and joy — and also the stress and anxieties — of human life. I have said that the purpose of life is to realise and ultimately reach union with the Ultimate Power, the origin and source of all life. How do we go about this. It's a very tall order. Let me say at the beginning very few actually achieve it. But it is in everyone to so do and in the fullness of time everyone will. Everyone has experienced at some time in their lives a glimpse of — how can I call it — a sense of timelessness — a morning's walk through the woods — a glorious sunset — the smile on your baby's face — the love in your lover's eyes — a sudden word here, a snatch from some old song, a line in a poem there — and finally holding the hand of your husband, wife or loved one lying dead upon the bed. These. poignant moments, when for a brief second, or maybe longer, when you are 'taken out of yourself' are pure and naked life, quite unlike anything you have experienced before. For that brief second you have reached union with the Divine. Then it recedes and you are back in the humdrum of normal existence. Some people, depending on its intensity, never forget the experience and it nags at them until eventually they are forced to do something about it. They have 'Awakened'. This is the first of the three states of the orthodox church's doctrine of the path to Realisation, although this is somewhat different from what is the teaching of the Ancient Wisdom. The three stages are — The Awakening — The Purification or Purgation — and finally The Realisation.

Let us look at Awakening.

Let me say, before I start, that the experience described above, which is the ultimate goal of life, can not be held continuously, for the human frame cannot hold it, it would break apart. But once the experience has been had to a sufficient degree it, can then form a backdrop to normal life which gives it a certainty and surety and freedom from stress and anxiety which would seem to be what the average westerner in this modern industrial technological world now seeks most. Books and courses now proliferate on how to seek harmony in one way or another with the anxieties of modern life. But it must be stressed while everyone seeks security there is no security. The only security is insecurity. Everything is in a constant state of change. While we live in this finite world we must adapt to constant change. The only state of changelessness is the Divine world. We can live, while still in this world, in a state of perfect peace and harmony with ourselves and with our neighbours and with no fear of the future, when we reach, on however small a scale, what is known as Realisation (the state mentioned above) or as Eugene Halliday would say, Reflexive Self Consciousness.

What exactly then is this state and how do we get it and what has it to do with awakening. Are we not awake already. Yes, of course, we are. But in what way are we awake. We are awake to the external world, the world of the senses, the world of things and events we see around us but at the same time we are completely unaware of our internal state. In this sense we are asleep. We get angry, we envy our neighbour his new car, we fancy the new girl on the check out. Do we know where these feelings and desires come from. And these feelings and desires and loves and hates govern all we do. We are slaves to them but in our ignorance think we are in control of who we are and what we do. But can you control them. You are swept along on their tide and often find yourself washed up and on the rocks. You then blame your predicament on something external, something outside yourself, whereas in reality it was you yourself who has caused it. You may not like the thought of this, but it is true.

When the merest hint of this comes into your mind, and when, possibly you have felt the experience of 'timelessness' mentioned above, and when in addition you have felt dissatisfied with your life so far and something must be done about it then, at that point, you have taken the first step to Awakening.

You are then on the path and if your resolve is firm you won't look back. What must you do now. Well, surprisingly, nothing. You do nothing, for you are already there. You are already perfect, you are already 'realised' but you do not know it. All you have to do is know it, that is all. So you do nothing. But can you do nothing. What is required in your doing nothing is simply realising who you really are.

For who you really are is not John Smith, or Mary Jones, not a separate being as such, but an integral part of that whole complex we call the universe. And this is the difficult bit. It is possible, but very rare, to 'realise' instantly, but apart from that, so yes, you have to do something.

The human being is said to be threefold, composed of spirit, soul and body. You are a spirit which is a soul in a body. The soul, which is what you actually are as a separate entity, is spirit which has entered a body and which it becomes for the course of that life. The spirit enters and identifies with this soul and body so as to discover through its experiences what it is and what it is capable of. This spirit is actually a kind of spark, or germ of the universal spirit which is — can I say — experimenting with itself and discovering itself and finding out what it can do. (Although the universal spirit, considered in itself as its essence and apart from its emergence as the universe remains always itself and unaffected by its involvement in the universe.) Yes, I know, it all sounds baffling, but remember the paradox. Life is not easily reasonable and logical, it is intuitional and, in the right frame of mind, can be understood with no problem. Life is paradox: black is white, hot is cold, it all depends on your point of reference. Life is relative. A pitch dark room is black, switch the light on and it is white, yet the room is exactly the same, it hasn't changed. Out in a freezing December day your hands feel cold, bring them together and blow on them and they warm up. In fact, the actual blowing is paradox, is the blowing process hot or cold. For you blow on you cold hands to warm them up and you blow on a hot cup of tea to cool it down

But this digresses. Although you are simply a spark of the universal spirit or life or fire, in yourself you feel a separate entity. This is true, you are a separate entity but — paradox again — you are also simply a spark doing the universal's will. This may sound disturbing but it is true. And the Awakening is the ultimately realising of this.

However, you may say, 'Simply a spark doing the universal's will. Am I. Am I not myself, doing my own will.' Yes, of course you are. And that is precisely the problem. Everyone is themselves doing their own will, hence clashes everywhere when will comes up against will — domestic arguments — parliamentary and business disputes — sports people, athletes, footballers and others fighting to be the greatest, the winner – civil wars – wars between nations – and finally the war to end all war and complete mutual self destruction. No wonder stress and anxiety is everywhere.

And it all starts with you. 'I am myself., doing my own will' So the Awakening begins by your asking yourself, 'Who is myself'. Are you really John Smith or Mary Jones. No. What you really are is a soul strung between spirit on the one hand and a body on the other. You can oscillate between the two. You can become more spiritual, you can become more body orientated. The spirit is your deep inner true self, your true, when realised, immortal self: your body is your false self, your temporary vehicle while you live in this incarnation for the purpose of manifestation, of having experiences and so developing. The spirit, being formless, needs form to discover itself. Another word for this spirit is pure consciousness. You are a consciousness. With this consciousness you look out upon the world. You see a tree.

Where is this tree. Is it 'out there'. Or is it in 'here'. In your consciousness. Think about this. The tree may be out there but, as far as you are concerned, it is in your consciousness. If you are not there to see it, suppose no one is there to see it, would it still be there. How do you know. Kant, the 17th century philosopher, said 'one can never know the thing as it is in itself, it is always understood through the prism of the observer'. One could easily say, 'No observer, no thing.' On an amusing note, there is the pair of limericks by Ronald Knox in which a young man in a quad, who finds it odd that a tree can still 'continue to be' if there is no one around, hears a reply from 'Yours Faithfully, God', to say that He is always around in the quad.

Eugene Halliday always stressed the phrase 'The Observer is not the Observed', by which he meant that if you can observe something you are not it, you are separate from it. The normal way is that in observing something or considering an idea, in that instant, you identify with the thing or idea. The thing you continually identify most with is your own body and your own thinking process so that you believe you are your body and thinking process. But if you can observe them, then you are not them, you are someone or something else. Who then are you. And this is the secret, the answer to which, gives Self Realisation. For you are really the hidden self, which is your real essence and the silent Watcher of all the actions and thoughts and desires of your false self and ego. The problem is that people think they are this ego and have forgotten their true self. This self is the big Self writ small. As such it is immune from all the troubles and anxieties of this war torn world. It watches over them, unperturbed, with a serene and calm gaze.

A young man, called Eckhart Tolle, had a breakdown at the age of 29. He had become so disillusioned with what seemed to him the meaninglessness of life and of what he perceived as his utter failure to achieve anything that he finally contemplated suicide. 'I'm a total failure. I can't live with myself any more.' Thinking thus, without warning, the strangest notion flashed through his mind. 'Who is this myself who can't live with me. There must be two of me.' He felt unable to dismiss this weirdest of thoughts and kept repeating it to himself. Suddenly all thought stopped and his mind became a total blank. He felt himself being drawn into some kind of vortex or void which seemed to be inside him rather than outside. Fear gripped him. He heard a voice which appeared to be inside his chest 'Resist nothing'. Eventually the fear ceased, he let go and fell into the void and lost consciousness. When he came to, everything was changed. Everything was as before but marvellously different. It was new and pristine as if new minted. Even the simple pencil on the table shone with a radiant light. He heard a bird on a tree outside the window and the song filled him with tears. The sheer wonder and loveliness of the world swept his heart and he knew he was a new and changed man. He stayed like this for about two years and then the ecstatic feeling slowly receded and he was his normal self again but full of a new zest for life which has never left him. He started to study the meaning of the experience and eventually became a spiritual teacher, which he still is. He now has an extensive website — just click on his name — and travels the world lecturing and talking to people. His first book was called 'The Power of Now'. A remarkable person and a perfect example of an 'instant' conversion but brought on after a prolonged period of stress, suffering and anxiety.

'Now'. This is a very important word. For there is only Now, only the Present. When you think about the Past you do so Now; when you think about the Future you do so Now. You cannot bring back the past. When you think about it or live it, it is only in your memory and your memory only occurs in the present moment. When you worry about some event in the future – which may or may not occur – the moment of worrying is now. It is all now. Everything happens now. You cannot ever get away from the now. Think of the immense age of the universe, millions upon millions of years. Think of the future of the universe, possibly also millions of years. As each moment occurs it occurs now. Life as we normally experience it consists of a continual succession of 'now' moments. This experience is the result of what we call Time. We live normally, except when we sleep, always in the Time world. And time is an illusion. It is a shadow of the Real world, Ultimate Reality, Eternity.

Sitting in a railway carriage travelling at 60 miles an hour or in a jet plane doing 500 miles an hour 6 miles up, the view from the window shows a succession of scenes passing one by one, those from the train passing rapidly, those from the plane, although it is travelling many times faster, much slower. It is all relative motion. If the curtain is closed and nothing is seen, although you are yourself travelling at 60 or 500 miles an hour you seem to be motionless. With the curtain open you experience Time which is passing, first Now, then behind the Past, and ahead the Future. With the curtain closed the sensation is stillness, it is all Now, with no sensation of motion. This feeling of 'All is Now.' is similar to Eternity – Time and Eternity are the two modes of Reality. We normally spend all our lives, except during sleep, in the Time aspect rushing hither and thither, bustle bustle and never residing in the Now, being oblivious of Eternity. The Time is the Something mode of Reality, the Now, Eternity, is the Nothing mode of Reality. By living in both simultaneously we are living in Total Reality. This is the Self Realisation – Eugene`s Reflexive Self Consciousness,

I will call it Resec from now on – which is the optimum state to be aimed at. However, these two, The Nothing and the Something are not two equal aspects of the one Reality, for the Nothing includes the Something in itself, more than the Something includes the Nothing. For you sitting in the railway carriage or the aeroplane the passing scene outside is an illusion for in so far as you merely observe it, you are not in it. For you the reality is your sitting apparently motionless in your seat. And you are doing this in the Now. The Now is the true reality from which, so to speak, you can never get out of, never escape from. To live in the Now is the Realisation of which I speak.

The ancient Greek oracle at Delphi had an injunction carved over its entrance, which goes back to prehistoric times and beyond, which was *gnothi seauton,* Know Thyself. This in two words, whether Greek or English, is the most important and vital piece of advice you can be given. Followed through it can save your life; ignored, you are, or can be, lost. (I speak here of your soul not your body. Remember you *are* a soul, your body is merely your vehicle.) So when I said earlier you need do nothing I was wrong. This you must do, or attempt to do. You won't fully succeed for it makes the climbing of Everest a mere doddle. But don't worry, even the greatest, even if they reach the summit, then find another higher height ahead. The true summit cannot be reached while you are still in this life. Just get as high as you can. But to have a go, realise its supreme importance for your happiness and well being and, in the last analysis, for the saving of your true self, your soul, no task can be more worthwhile. 'For what shall it profit a man if he shall gain the whole world and lose his own soul' (Mark 8:36). And it is an interesting absorbing task that can be fun. It involves watching of yourself at all times, becoming aware of the often absurd and truly hilarious and stupid mistakes you frequently make. Of seeing yourself as two people, one the actor, the other the audience, the Silent Watcher. This actor has to be got under control for it doesn't know what it is doing half the time. Five minutes of real self-observance will prove this. This actor, this doer and thinker, is your self-will, your personal self that you think is all you really are, your false ego. You are a million times more than this, you are an immortal and spiritual soul that can have the world at your feet when you realise this. But here a paradox arises. When you have the world at your feet, if you have been true to yourself, sincere and honest with yourself and have, if only partially, conquered your lower self and had a glimmering of what it feels like to be your true self, then you find you no longer want the world at your feet. It can stay where it was and you find you just enjoy watching it and being in it and it is more wonderful and vibrant than ever you thought possible.

This brings me to yet another paradox. 'You find you just enjoy watching it'.

How can you do that when you are watching yourself the whole time. This paradox fooled me for a very long time. I went about watching myself, trying not to use a word unless I knew its true meaning, analysing my every thought and action, as Eugene taught, and so became more introverted than usual, stiff and awkward, restricted in my whole life and in my behaviour towards others. I felt inhibited, afraid to move or speak for fear of falling into some dreadful hole. Yet at the same time here was Eugene's own behaviour – a man who taught we need to know the meaning of every word we use and to watch ourselves at all times – totally relaxed and easy, responding immediately and fluently to every request and situation, fully in command of himself. At one point he said he never knew what he was going to say until he said it. I was completely knocked out and didn't know whether I was coming or going. How could he be so in command of himself and yet didn't know what he was saying until he heard the words coming out of his mouth. This was the paradox. It took me ages to realise he was actually living in the Nothing and the Something at the same time. He was a fully realised man, living where Spirit and Matter were One. At one point he said to me, 'I have no ego'. He had conquered his lower self, his false ego so it no longer exercised its hold over him. Rather he exercised his hold over it. I took a lesson from this. For he exercised his hold easily, with no effort. This, I later found, is the spirit of Zen. Take it easy. Relax. Enjoy yourself. Zen teaches carrying on in a strange, relaxed, unhurried and easy way, while yet possessed of the necessary intensity and 'tone'. I found, when I got it right, I was wonderfully light-headed. I felt like a baby, but a wise baby. Eyes wide open, fully alert, watchful, not letting go of anything, yet not holding on to anything. There is an old saying which expresses it well, 'Let go, let God'.

The main source of the Zen philosophy is that great classic, the Chinese Tao Te Ching. This expresses in 81 short – what can I call them – poems, aphorisms, epigrams, paradoxes – statements which are bewilderingly and teasingly ambivalent, and enigmatic, about the origin of life and its meaning for humans. They have foxed European sinologists for centuries. There are said to be over 30 English translations. I had a go myself. I have no knowledge of Chinese. My method of translation was to lay a dozen English versions alongside one another and compare one with the other. Each was completely different from the others. The best of the translators, Walter Gorn Old, wrote, 'There can be little doubt that any translation from the Chinese is capable of extreme flexibility, of which indeed, the translator must avail himself if he would rightly render the spirit rather than the letter of the text; and the spirit, after all, is the essential thing if we follow the teaching of Lao Tzu. It is safe to say that the more literal the translation may be the more obscure its meaning'. Here then, for I think it is relevant, is my version of No 17 of the Tao:

> A man is most free exerting not his will over lower impulses
> Not so free when they obey him as a beloved master.
> Less free when they obey him as a feared master.
> Least free when ignoring him they go their ways.
> Only his lifting can raise them.
> Gently he does it, not violencing himself.
> Then, as higher impulses, so gentle has been the pull,
> They think it has been their own will.
> Thus no Will need be exerted upon them.

So keep on working, but take it easy. Enjoy it

So to sum up. The coming to be is the Awakening from your usual normal state of existence, with its troubles, uncertainties, depressions, stresses and anxieties, to the realisation that there is a better way of existence, a higher way of living, which is harmonious with every aspect of the world and the people, animals and the environment around you and which brings peace, lack of all stress, contentment, and a positive certainty you are, in essence, an immortal soul moving, however slowly, onwards and upwards to an ever more glorious and wonderful future. This way of living is by living in the ever present Now.

In one sense living in the Now is simple. You just decide to do it and then you do it. However, for most of us it is not so simple. You find you have to work at it. And then, after a while laziness, lassitude, no signs of progress, doubts creep in and then your efforts tail off and finally cease. I can't help here. All I can say is 'don't give up'. The smallest possible effort will bring results. It is often said one can never make much progress on one's own, one needs a teacher. There is an old saying, 'When the pupil is ready the Master will appear'. Believe this. He did for me. And I found his mere presence was enough to convince me. I knew beyond all peradventure, and for which I knew I would die rather than deny him, that he spoke truth. Once I grasped the deeper meaning of what his message was I was off. I no longer needed him. He had showed me the way and henceforward I knew I could proceed on my own. He said at one point, 'My job is done when you no longer need me'. If you are never fortunate enough to find a teacher then you must become your own teacher, you must become an autodidact, i.e., someone who is self taught, through books for instance. From nowhere and sometimes in the most unlikely circumstances the book will appear that will provide just what you need. Or you may meet a friend who suggests a meeting you should go to or something he's seen on the internet. The opportunities and possibilities are endless. The only requirement is that you remain firm in your resolve. The rest will follow. However one proviso. You mustn't go about waiting for it. Just live your life as normally and then when you least expect it something will happen. It may even come from inside yourself. Something may without warning flash through your mind that is the answer to a problem that's been holding you back. But I ask you to believe, and I speak from experience, that once you decide to embark on what some call 'The Work', although I don't like the term as it suggests unpleasant effort that puts many off when it should be exciting and rewarding, you will get help from the Supreme Spirit that watches over all. This Spirit is indeed waiting for such as yourself to come along, for his intention is for everyone to finally be 'Realised' for when they are they will work for Him instead of merely for themselves. The beauty of all this is that when you work for Him you find that it also helps you, for you find your life immeasurably enhanced and that you henceforth live in the 'peace that passes all understanding'.

One last thing. I said earlier that the next state after the Awakening is the Purification. A brief word on that and then I am done and the rest is up to you. Purification means that as you progress, that is if you are doing it honestly and not for some ignoble cause say, lording it over your fellows, you find you are growing ever more unselfish, less seeking always your own pleasures at the expense of others, less seeking to escape what pains come your way. You will be moving towards achieving a state which the ancients called – and they meant it somewhat differently from what it means today – Virtue. This means being wholly trustworthy, honest, totally unselfish, always ready to help our neighbour and so on. It means 'purifying' your self. This is essential.  You may find others around you may accuse you of selfishness, of always thinking of yourself, whereas, in truth, you are actually doing the opposite.  These others don't realise that in order to help others you must first help yourself, or rather, know yourself. 'First cast out the beam out of thine own eye and then thou shalt see clearly to cast out the mote out of thy brother's eye (Matt. 7:5) This is called Enlightened Self Interest.

The Way is the way towards your own perfection.  (And remember, any such perfection increases that in the world.  Every tiny improvement is noticed.)  Once experienced you will be satisfied with nothing less. Once experienced nothing can hold you back.

### Part Three. Being. The Return.

Being is the true state of every individual.  The individual initially exists only in a latent and potential state before the universe comes into existence. He sleeps peacefully, unformed and naked, in the bosom of the deep, that deep of the sleeping Being that is the Infinite Power in its sleep mode, called by Eastern tradition the Night of Brahma or *Pralaya.*  When the Day of Brahma arrives, named *Manvantara,* the Infinite Power awakes, the universe is born and all the latent entities that are within it are born anew and begin their immensely long journey from their spiritual home and down from the mountain heights, through the valley of shadows, through joy and sorrow, down into materiality in order to develop themselves so as to ultimately return back to their home, fully realised beings and gods, where their Father joyously awaits them.  It is the parable of the Prodigal Son and every man and woman must tread it, as must indeed every living thing, for evolution proceeds everywhere and ultimately the whole universe and all living things will be welcomed in this way by their Father.  All Life will truly become that Infinite Sphere with its centre everywhere and its circumference nowhere. This is the story of the world, as it is the story of the individual, night and day following each other in the being's life, as the Day and Night of Brahma follow each other in the universe's life. Life is eternal, it has no beginning or end, it will always be. The universe will always be: the realised being will always be. By going down into the valley of experience and back up again man and woman come to realise who they are and have become masters of themselves and fully responsible and self determining beings. The son who never left home is pure and whole but doesn't know it: the son who returns is pure and whole but does know it. He is first involved, then evolved, he has developed. The son who stayed at home has not developed. This is the story of the world, to develop, to evolve, to move from Becoming to fully developed Being. No one, in one lifetime, can reach this position, it will take many lives, but no matter how slowly the sooner one starts to take oneself in hand the better. For one at once starts to find a purpose, to leave behind all the stress and anxieties which normally beset one and to find peace and harmony. One brings oneself into line with the great rhythmic cycles and movement of the vast universe and one experiences the strangest. yet most beautiful and utterly ineffable feeling of pure and sublime Love for all beings and all creation, for one knows one is oneself all beings and all creation.

This is Being. This is Self Realisation. This is the state of knowing that one's little self is identical with and one with the Big Self that is the Intelligent Source that is the origin of the universe and is the universe. As already mentioned Eugene's phrase for this state is Resec – Reflexive Self Consciousness – and his short book of that name gives the best explanation I know of exactly what this state is and how to reach it. I cannot pretend to emulate his marvellously precise and lucid style and method of explanation. All I can say is that he describes the essentials for obtaining resec. He shows how to realise you must break identification with all objects, especially your own body, for otherwise you become a slave to them, which is the position of the normal person. Freedom comes when you realise you are not an object, not your body, you are consciousness itself, and consciousness is not a thing, it is that in which objects are seen, it is the observer that observes the object. Consciousness is formless, it is the Nothing which is aware of the Something. As thus it is Free. Freedom is when you are free from identification with all form.  However, the forms don't then disappear, nothing changes, the world is still as it always was.  It is simply that you see it differently.  As William Blake said, 'The fool sees not the same tree the wise man sees'.  Now when you are in this state, aware of the Nothing and the Something simultaneously, you discover the world has become miraculously alive and vibrant, every smallest thing becomes 'holy' as Blake said.  He also said 'To see eternity in a grain of sand and heaven in a wild flower'.

Eugene doesn't mention how it *feels* to be in this state, he simply describes how to reach it.  Now this state, which is a feeling state, not an intellectual one — although the intellectual aspect comes in later in attempting to evaluate its significance — has many degrees, varying from the merest glimpse to the most intense.  The merest glimpse is experienced when sensing the beauty of a glorious sunset, or walking through an avenue of trees in a forest and feeling the strange and often sinister awe and fear that comes over one by the mystery of the trees hedging you in closely on every side.  People on holiday sitting and looking at the ocean, after a few moments, nearly always experience a feeling of serenity and peace coupled with wonder at the limitless immensity of the ocean spread out before them and a momentary sense of the mystery of all life and their insignificance in it.  I think almost everyone has had these momentary glimpses at some time during their lives.  These feelings move up by imperceptible degrees to the most intense, where the whole being seems to be swept up into an indescribable condition of union with the All, an ineffable state often called Ecstasy or Rapture.  Midway between the two states exists the one which, being the halfway point, can exist as the background to one`s life.  The momentary glimpse is too brief to have any lasting effects — though in some cases it may do so — the most intense being what is so overwhelming it cannot be sustained for any period of time for it would break the being.  Eugene, I think, concentrated on this midway point, his whole teaching was on the pupil achieving resec as a continuous background to one's life.

Speaking for myself, I have not achieved resec, not fully anyway.  I have had many momentary glimpses and I have experienced four occasions of degrees of intensity which have now enabled me to live my life with such a certainty and sureness that I am in the fortunate position of living in harmony and peace with myself and my fellow man and indeed of all creation. I do not yet fully know myself but I feel I am well on the way.

I would like to write now of these four experiences. I have briefly mentioned odd bits of some of them in my small booklets, but I would like to go now into more detail, if that is possible, for it is so difficult to try and express the quality of an experience that is so far beyond the average everyday experience of daily life. It may help others who may be struggling with the same problem.

The first occasion came long ago in 1935 when I was ten years old. Although that is now eighty years ago, the memory is still as fresh as ever. I stood alone one evening in the garden of our London home and looked up at the night sky. Here the street lights were far away and the sky was black and a myriad of tiny lights twinkled back at me. I gazed at them in boyish wonderment, marvelling at the immensity of the universe and the mystery of life. I remained motionless thus for perhaps five minutes and then a feeling, an odd thought, began to sweep through me until it at last engulfed my whole being and I became rigid with the weirdest mixture of awe and fear coupled with a feeling, a powerful sense of longing to know. 'Why is there a world. What does it all mean. The obvious thing is for there to be nothing, not something. I am alive, the stars are alive, Why. Who could have invented it. What a strange thing to invent. *Why is there life.* Nothing is the most natural thing.' I stood there transfixed by the weirdness of existence.

Eventually a call came from the house for supper, then a further call, and then a sharply insistent call and in a daze, not knowing who I was, I went back into the house. Now clearly it is commonplace to look up at the night sky and the stars and feel this sense of wonderment, millions have done it, but for this boy of ten the intensity and – the only word I can think of – *weirdness* of the experience stayed with him and it is still with me at 91. So for all these years there has been this burning desire to know, to discover the meaning of life. It took me many years to realise that more than mere knowledge is needed. Knowledge is only part of the story, not even the most important part. What is more influential is feeling, intuition, gut feeling, the imperative to *live* what you know. To know that two plus two equals four is a fact but it doesn't change your behaviour. To know, to *understand, to intuit,* the meaning of life requires more than mere knowledge, for mere knowledge allows you to say, 'Yes, I understand that' and then carry on your life as normal. To truly understand the meaning of life you have to experience it, and then know it, then *be* it. Without experiencing it you do not truly understand it. This, in truth, applies to understanding anything. Knowledge, by which I mean, rationality, the ability to reason is not creative, it simply compares one thing with another in order to reach a conclusion. This is logic. Understanding, on the other hand, means to feel as well as to know. It means to experience, to *be* what is known.

---

The second occasion occurred, as far as I can recall, in 1948 or 9. I had come out of the Royal Navy, had trained as an actor, and was now in a production of Cinderella at the Arts Theatre in Cambridge. One afternoon I wandered into the Fitzwilliam Museum. At the end of an aisle I saw an immense statue, some twelve feet or more tall of a naked man standing and holding a club. I thought he was Hercules. I went up close and gazed in awe at his huge figure towering over me. Idly, I rested my hand on one of his feet. Immediately, a sensation passed through my whole body. I felt his blood flow in a continuous stream from him to me. We became a continuum, there was no separation. The ancient Greek world and I were one, yet I still remained myself. It was most strange. I felt Time stretching in a continuous uninterrupted line from him to me. I knew him as he knew me. We were one, a unity. Yet I was alive and breathing and he was just a statue. Yet between us passed a living stream of vibrant life. I can still feel this now as I write it.

So what had happened. I do not know. Had I tuned in to what is known as the Akashic records, or what the Bible calls The Book of Life. Possibly. To quote dear old Will Shakespeare, 'There are more things in heaven and earth, Horatio,. than are dreamed of in your philosophy'. The point is the intensity of this feeling of actually experiencing this living and continuous stream in which there is no separation between him and me, just this living vibrant life. It was an experience like the earlier one, which was of the weirdness of existence, yet different somehow in quality, that of empathy, of love for the oneness of things.

---

The third occasion, far more powerful and intense, occurred on February $2^{nd}$ 1985 just two months into my $61^{st}$ year. During the intervening years I had, among many other things, become an ocean yachtsman. So now, here I was with two fellow sailors delivering a wealthy man's yacht from Majorca in the Mediterranean to Corpus Christie in Texas, a journey which took 60 days at sea and covered 6,200 nautical miles. We had sailed through the Med and on to the Canary Islands, where we stocked up on food water and fuel, crossed the Atlantic to Antigua in 29 days, thence through the Caribbean in 19 days and were now on the last leg in the Gulf of Mexico. On the last day, within about 60 miles of our destination, we experienced a Northerly Buster, a fierce wind that is common in the Gulf.

I quote now from my log, 'It is now howling from the NW. We are steering about 280. We hurriedly lash Big Daddy along the rail and hoist the main, putting in the second reef. We are soaked and sweating. Unbelievably the seas are already 15 feet high. In about 20 minutes. (We have the main up as the wind is on the nose and we don't want to lose ground.) The rest of the night was total misery. Freezing cold and the ship bouncing horribly. When the day dawned and we saw the seas, my heart sank. The highest I have ever seen. Huge walls of water, spume running down their sides like spittle on an old man's beard. We crashed unmercifully and many times I feared for the rigging. The noise and howling of the wind was terrible. Yet strangely I was never frightened. I watched it all fascinated. We were so near yet so far.'

So here I was now, taking the morning watch, and I sat alone at the helm, my two companions taking a well earned rest, asleep down below. The wind stayed at 30 to 40 knots yet I could see the worst was over and the seas were beginning to die down. Though they were still enormous, the crests often towering over us almost to the height of the mast. We rode them like a horse up a series of hills, up, up we went, hovered on the crest a moment, during which I saw to the horizon, then down into the trough, during which I saw only walls of blue green water. A roller coaster ride! Steering required concentration, one false move could spell disaster. No place for novices.

It was a magnificent morning, with a splendid sun, a clear blue sky of the purest azure, and as the yacht rose to the top of the waves I saw the majesty of the sea spread out before me, with the sun running across the wave tops with their dazzling white crests and catching the water droplets in thousands of tiny rainbows. Then down again into the cavern of water from which I feared she would never rise but carry on down into the very depths but up the splendid beast would always rise and then the magnificent sea and sky and sun again. I cried aloud at the unutterable beauty and grandeur and majesty of the scene. How could anyone live and see such power. What did life matter. I had seen such beauty – let me die now – nothing after this had value. How long I was in this state I do not know – subsequently I blessed the fact I was an experienced seaman and sailed the yacht well, though was quite unaware of so doing, and did not let my sleeping companions down – maybe half an hour but it could have been a second, it was timeless – but during this time feelings swept through me of such power I thought my frame would give and I would die. I wanted to die. Yet I was so full of joy. Yet it was not ordinary joy. It was also full of sadness. It would be better to say it was not either, but that it rose above them, it was at a different level, a new dimension obtained. But these are all words. The experience was ineffable, indescribable, no words can describe it, it was beyond words. As I gazed at this scene of sheer awesome power, which was unutterably beautiful, I knew that I was nothing, absolutely nothing. But I was not nothing, I was everything. I was me, I was the yacht, I was the sea, I was the sky, I was the wind. They were all one. But they were not all one. Only the awareness was there. And this awareness was so vibrant, so beautiful, so full of life and yet though nothing was there everything was there. There was everything, there was nothing, all merging into one yet all remaining itself. All was not one yet not two. I know this reads like the ramblings of an idiot but it is all I can say.

I was more alive than I had ever been. I was full of love for all and everything and everyone. I felt I had at last found reality. I felt I had at last come into my real self, my true self. I laughed, I cried, I was silent and just watched.

I found in reading again my log, which had lain unread in the drawer for thirty years, there was no mention of the experience except the last words already quoted, 'Yet strangely I was never frightened. I watched it all fascinated. We were so near yet so far'. Perhaps somehow it was too sacred to be mentioned, too sacred to be profaned by words. I didn't know who might read the log on my return. Writing of it now there came a thought that I had never thought of before. The experience 'came out of the blue', literally as well as metaphorically, sudden and unprepared for. Yet I see now I had been unconsciously preparing for it during sixty days at sea, sixty days during which I had observed the ocean in all its moods, from calm and serene to full of sound and fury, above all inscrutable, mysterious, revealing nothing yet revealing everything. Peter Pye, who also sailed the ocean, wrote 'In the moods and silences of a great ocean there lies an uncertainty like a question mark that is the reflection of life itself'. So the experience was not sudden and unasked for but the natural culmination of the voyage – 'We were so near yet so far'. In a sense the natural culmination of the voyage of life itself. I think of Eckhart Tolle and his sudden breakdown after a long period of stress and strain and feelings of failure. My experience followed in the same vein except it came suddenly after a period of, not feelings of failure, but calmly after a period of endurance. I read in my log, the very last words I wrote on the voyage, 'Truly it is a very wonderful world we live in'.

---

The fourth occasion, which was not a single incident but a prolonged one, began in 1990 when I was 65 and lasted intermittently for three years. This was the deepest, most intense period interspersed with dull periods of my whole life. At its completion I knew I was changed.

What did this period involve. On the surface nothing really, none of my family noticed any difference in my behaviour but beneath I was slowly being torn to pieces and then remade anew. Yet in a strange way this is not exactly a true statement. In most ways I didn't change at all for I had always been like it. I can only say what happened was a kind of culmination, a sort of bringing out into the open — in the open for me at least — what had always lain dormant within me. At the end I knew where I stood where before I has been semi-consciously staggering towards it.

It was a love affair but not an ordinary love affair. I never kissed her, there was nothing carnal about it all, it was completely spiritual. And it remained unrequited throughout. To her I was a lifelong friend no more, yet for me she was a catalyst, changing me yet remaining unchanged herself.

She was a sailing friend and one day we went for a walk along the cliffs near our respective homes. She was a country woman and pointed out to me things I never knew, the names of various wild flowers, how to spot badger holes and so on. Some time later I was going through some photos and came across several of her sitting on those same cliffs and smiling into the camera. As I sat looking, something about that smile, something about the expression in her eyes, something about her dimple, something, in fact, about her whole expression came over me in a wave of love, impersonal love. It wasn't love directed at me — I must have been the one who took the snaps — it was a strange impersonal love, it was simply love itself. Love that was, well, loving itself. She was the bearer of love, absolute love. Whether this odd feeling that encompassed my whole being came from her or whether it came from me and projected on to her I do not know. All I know I felt I was looking into the eyes of absolute Love itself. I sat there thunderstruck. for how long I do not know. I seemed to be transported to another timeless reality. Later I wrote a sonnet which I gave to her and she said she liked it. And so the three year period began. We both taught weekly evening classes in seamanship and navigation at the local art college and often I would give her my latest sonnet. In all I wrote sixty love sonnets which she always accepted with her lovely smile, which went straight up my spine, but without any comment and so we parted. (I later privately published them in a small edition of fifty copies.)

(A digression here on sonnets and why I write them. I have written many as I find the form congenial to my temperament. There are two types, the Petrarchian and the Shakespearean. I use the latter. It consists of fourteen lines of ten syllables each with the accent on the second syllable as thus di Da, di Da, di Da, and so on. The fourteen lines consist of three quatrains with the rhyme as thus AC–BD. The poem is rounded off with a rhyming couplet which sums up the whole. All art – and I don't profess my sonnets to be such, although of course one should always aim for the highest – requires form and structure, often quite rigid, in order to attempt to express, or at least suggest, the formless, the inexpressible which lies behind all phenomena, and which I take to be the function of art. Some such forms in music are the fugue, the concerto, the sonata, the symphony and so on. Poetry has as well as the sonnet, the ode, the elegy, the hymn and the ballad. In painting a number of basic principles, as the law of Unity, the law of Echo and the all important ratio of The Golden Mean called in Greek *phi* which is found everywhere in Nature and expresses the ratio, the short line is to the long line as the long line is to the sum of both, as 5 is to 8 as 8 is to 13. You find the Golden Mean everywhere in the Renaissance paintings of the great Italian Masters. It expresses harmony and is thus most pleasing to the eye. Most modern art is ugly in the eyes of many as it ignores this ratio as it often ignores all law.)

Here is one of my Sonnets of Love, No. 9

> When I say 'I love you', what do I mean.
> Who is it in reality I love.
> Is it just you as you, or have I seen
> Reflections of a Greater Love above.
> Your smile, which first I loved in you, is you
> Unique and like no other smile I've known
> And yet, while you, I glimpse a broader view
> A Cosmic Smile behind it and not shown.
> So you are you, and yet you are not you,
> A seeming paradox so strange yet true,
> For Cosmic Smile needs windows to smile through

And when it does its smile and yours aren't two.
So yes, I love that Greater Love it's true,
Yet when I say 'I love you' I love *you*.

In the periods between writing the sonnets I felt dull and listless, carrying on my daily tasks normally but without much zest or enthusiasm. Then something would occur, some apparently innocent incident, something heard or something seen on TV, anything, and this would bring a word or maybe a whole line into my mind of a fresh sonnet and I would be away. Then I became — how can I say — heated, and nothing mattered but the new sonnet. I would wrestle with it all day, sometimes two or three, and I was in an unaccountable way, possessed, caught up in an impersonal world of Absolute Love. Yet, when the sonnet was finished it was intensely personal, full of love for that one person while yet in and behind it can be seen the impersonal Love for that Greater Love which was the love of the infinite unknowable power for itself, the same impersonal love I had first seen in her eyes. She was herself and yet was greater than herself. She was the expression of the Something and the Nothing. Later I realised she was the Beatrice to my Dante, Laura to my Petrarch, Isis the White Goddess to my Apuleius. Shortly, she was my Muse.

The only phrase I can think of that does its best to describe how I felt when writing the sonnets is 'timeless reality'. I slowly realised, no, I knew all along, it was the same feeling as in the previous three experiences. Each time I was caught up into a new dimension, a whole new way of seeing things, a whole new way of life that was 'timeless'. I knew for that brief moment I was living in Absolute Reality, Absolute Love, which transcended both Good and Evil, or rather there was no Good or Evil, only Love. Love was all. It is the strangest, unbearable feeling which I called in another sonnet 'exquisite pain'. And whereas in the first three experiences it was a single brief moment, in writing the sonnets it came with every time of writing. I was blessed — rewarded. I know not — with the ineffable experience sixty times. Then slowly they faded with 'a dying fall' as I wrote my last sonnet and have so far not returned. But I gained a creative surge which, after nearly thirty years, is with me still. I wrote a novel and over thirty of my small booklets each of which I privately published. I am still going strong with no sign of easing off.

      I have now settled down into a serene and quiet retirement in which I feel purposeful and positive, happy and content, still busy learning, and above all filled with love for all and everyone and everything. As I wrote at the end of my Atlantic log, 'Truly it is a very wonderful world we live in.' Here is the last sonnet I wrote, No 60.

> Our chaste and snow white love has settled down,
> We rest together in a tranquil sea.
> In gentle sun-kissed waters do we drown
> Where, wordless, I am you and you are me.
> What bliss it is to know and have such love
> So quiet and timeless where no stress is there.
> Where each is other's hand in other's glove,
> Where each is other's joy each other's care.
> We do not need to meet each ev'ry day,
> Mere space, time, and distance does not sever.
> A thousand miles between — there's no 'away'
> For us it's all before, now, and forever.
> Our love lies like a lamb in our heart's core
> So pure and sweet we need desire no more.

---

# Book 2

# WHAT IS ENLIGHTENMENT

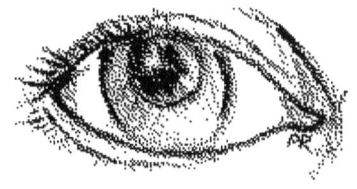

What has already gone we call the PAST;
The FUTURE comes to all of us at last;
But at the moment of its living through,
All time is of the PRESENT to our view.

Enlightenment, as it is used here, refers to a transcendent state of being, of heightened consciousness, of increased awareness that very few attain to and yet if attained bestows the freedom that all of us aspire to, the freedom to be in control of one's life, to live in perfect harmony with nature and all one's fellow creatures, and above all to be always in a state of perfect – *peace that passes all understanding*.

Quite a tall order! Who, if any, in this world of toil, conflict and suffering, can be said to exist in such a state? Has anyone ever reached this supreme state of being, and if so, how?

Since ancient times, spiritual teachers of all traditions have taught this as the highest of human aspirations and have pointed out the way of achievement.

The method is extremely simple yet extremely hard to do.

In a nutshell, one must die to one's lower self and thus release a higher and truer self. This self is eternal and knows all things. This self is the true self of the being and is one with all of life. But it is normally covered over with the busy–busy, practical, mundane, time–obsessed, false self that is usually called the *ego*.

There are many recorded accounts of people in situations of extreme danger where suddenly they hear a voice, sometimes in their own heads, sometimes outside of themselves, taking over and telling them what to do. Often they are aware of another phantom stranger alongside them encouraging and advising them. These beings, these voices, are never wrong.

Who, or what, are they?

Shortly, they are the higher, the truer, self of the being, who is 'above the fray' and is thus able to correctly appraise the situation and decide the appropriate response. It is the silent watcher behind, or in, every human being and who is, in fact, the true essence of that being.

Much recent research has been done on the two hemispheres of the brain, the *bicameral* brain. The left hemisphere, which by crossover affects the right side, governs analytical reasoning processes. It is, *per se*, non creative, but acts by comparing existing alternatives. It is generally considered to be male orientated, and is responsible for the amazing technology of the modern world.

The right hemisphere, affecting the left side, on the contrary is non rational, is creative and imaginative. It is generally considered to be female orientated and is responsible for most art and activities with an aesthetic input.

Put another way, the left side separates, analyses and is partial. The right side combines, synthesizes and is holistic.

All human beings, of course, have both these characteristics, but in the modern world the left hemisphere has gradually become not only the dominant half but, one can almost say, the only half. Right halvers, females, artists, imaginative thinkers, creative thinkers, lateral thinkers, have had progressively less and less say in the moulding of societies. Only in primitive and indigenous societies has this not been the case.

In prehistoric times, in the Golden Age, the brain was truly bicameral; both sides were equally balanced and played off one against the other. If there was any imbalance it was that the Goddess, the female, ruled. Now, in the evolutionary scheme of things it has become necessary for the left side, the man, to become dominant in order to master the material world. For thousands of years we have had a patriarchal society. But now it has gone too far. We desperately need to regain total balance. Otherwise, the left side, man, unredeemed will destroy the world. (That will not truly matter in the cosmic scheme, for life will just pick itself up and produce new life forms, but we will no longer be here to pick ourselves up!)

So what has all this to do with enlightenment?

Enlightenment comes when the right side is allowed its rightful place. The right side is the holistic side. It is in no way separate from the whole of creation, while the left side is the ego side, the feeling of the individual that he is separate from all creation. Both sides are necessary, of course, but if one side gets out of kilter then the being is in conflict with himself and pain and suffering is the result.

In the Western world, which is the most affected by the left side dominance, many teachers have arisen as to how to rebalance and produce harmony and peace in the individual and thus in the world. One of the problems is that the ordinary man does not realise he is in need of help — is in fact asleep — is in need of saving. He thinks his present position is the normal one. He gets up, goes to work, returns, often has disputes with his workmates, and more often with his wife at home, has worries about money, redundancy *etc*, and is in constant anxiety and fear about his prospects and the dire state of the world. He lives in a perpetual state of apprehension, only relieved by a yearly holiday in order to relax, merely to find he's carried his troubles and cares with him.

Enlightenment eliminates all this. So what do the teachers say?

As mentioned earlier the problem has been recognised since earliest times. Mystics, Christian saints, yogis, shamans, rishis, avatars, Zen masters, philosophers *et al* have all given in their various tongues, cultures and historic periods the same answer. Modern teachers do the same.

Put simply, the villain of the piece is the mind.

The Western man identifies with his mind and thinks it is him. But it is not him.

It is simply a tool he uses to make sense of the world. The mind is like a marvellous computer that is never switched off, churning out data constantly. The ordinary man is identified with this mind and is thus continually being whirled hither and thither by its never ending motions. The thoughts of the average man totally control him. Sit in a chair and try to stop thinking. You find it impossible. You think *you* are thinking. But are you? Are not the thoughts thinking you?

Try an experiment. Instead of thinking the thoughts, step aside and just watch the thoughts. Let them come and go without interference and just watch them. You immediately become aware there are two of you, the one thinking and the one watching the thinking.

One of the greatest of modern teachers, Eugene Halliday, in his seminal book, *Reflexive Self-Consciousness,* gives a marvellously simple and helpful mantra – 'The Observer is not the Observed'. Anything you can observe is not you, so if you can observe your thinking process you are not that thinking process. Once you realise you are not the thinking you are released from the thinking and all its attendant anxieties, futile anticipations and fears.

Then try watching your emotions; your anger, hatreds, loves, pains, pleasures. Once again, just letting them happen but observing the while releases you from them.

This, in essence, is all there is to enlightenment. But easier said than done. Your thoughts and feelings constitute all you have ever considered as your self, your sense of identity, and they don't give up without a fight and will pull you back time and time again. Yet persistence wins out in the end.

Yet now a strange piece of advice. Don't strive, don't struggle, don't make a battle out of it. Don't say things like, 'I'm halfway there, soon I'll make it'. If you do, you'll never make it, for the mind will seize on the striving and turn it around and use it for its own purposes, bolstering up your false sense of ego. You do not progress towards enlightenment; you are either enlightened or you are not. An electric light is either on or off. Jesus said, 'My yoke is easy and my burden is light'. So take it easy, let it happen. As the saying is, *Let go, let God*

Most people have felt the strange feeling of bliss and peace that comes over them when seeing a splendid sunset, or on a walk through the woods, with the sun slanting through the trees, hearing a sudden heart-stopping bird call. A sense of total unity, of oneness with all life sweeps over one. One feels one could live in this moment for ever. But such moods are usually brief and fade almost before they have begun. They are often referred to as *peak experiences* and many are described in William James's famous book, *The Varieties of Religious Experience*. Such moments are what is meant by enlightenment.

Can one experience bliss constantly?

Well, if you practise watching your thoughts, watching your feelings; in those moments when you are suddenly aware of such watching, you are in the *present* moment of true being, of enlightenment. Such moments, brief as they are, gradually become more frequent, gradually become longer, and over a period of time can become continuous.

*In the present.* That is the answer. For enlightenment means to live in the present moment. If you think of it, there is only this present moment, only the *now*. Most people live either in the past or in an imagined future. Yet the past and the future are illusions, they do not exist. The past exists for you only as a memory. When you remember the past and live in it, you are doing so now. And the future only exists as a projected anticipatory pleasure or a dreaded possibility. When you dwell in it you are doing so now. And when it finally comes it is now. The whole of life consists of a continuous *now* moment. To live in this moment, to be acutely aware that you only exist in this present moment, is to live truly in the fullness of being, to experience the joy and ineffable delight in the wonder and glory of the sheer splendour of all life going on in ever increasing newness. *When the morning stars sang together, and all the sons of God shouted for joy.*

Life is a continual *Now.* There is no past and no future, for the past is a now that has occurred and the future is a now that will occur. The present now is a result of past nows, and the future will be the result of present nows. The now is all there is. So live in the now. Living in the now is enlightenment. An excellent book on this is Eckhart Tolle's *The Power of Now.*

Enlightenment is ineffable and cannot be described in words, but must be experienced. When experienced, however briefly, you know beyond peradventure what it is. And you know that you know, and no amount of pseudo scientific antagonism will persuade you otherwise. It cannot be described in words yet many have attempted to have some sort of shot at it. Here are a few.

1. *Quality.* The definition of Robert M Persig in *Zen and the Art of Motor Cycle Maintenance*

2. *Presence.* Many writers, but especially Eckhart Tolle in *The Power of Now.*

3. *Essence.* Gurdjieff. See his marvellous description of the Afghan warrior in *Tales of Remarkable Men.*

4. *Being.* Many writers. They all talk of the essential aspect of just being fully alive to one's existence.

5. *Reflexive Self-Consciousness.* Eugene Halliday. His book of the same title gives, I think, the most exhaustive and concise treatment of the subject.

6. *Self Remembering.* Ouspensky, a pupil of Gurdjieff. In *In Search of the Miraculous* he gives a fascinating account of wandering through a Russian city and trying to remember himself — *i.e.* stay fully in the present, the now — and succeeding briefly only to fail again.

7. *The Now.* Eckhart Tolle. *The Power of Now.*

8. *No Mind. Suchness.* Zen Buddhism. Zen repays close study.

9. *The Noble Eightfold Path.* The Buddha.

10. *Practice of the Presence of God.* Letters of Brother Lawrence. The Medieval approach and terminology, but dealing with exactly the same Experience.

11. *Impeccability.* The Don Juan books. The way of the spiritual warrior, beautifully described by Carlos Castaneda.

12. *The Holy Grail. Chivalry. The Arthurian Ideal.* The search for the Holy Grail is the search for the essence of Being

13. *Noblesse Oblige. The Gentleman.* The gentleman acts always from Being, behaving perfectly under all conditions.

14. *The Kingdom of Heaven.* Jesus Christ, who says everything there is to say about finding the Kingdom, which is Being, which is Life Eternal.

---

Lastly, it is called by :—

    The ancient Egyptians, *Maat*

    The Chinese, the *Tao.*

    The Hindu, *Samadhi.*

    The Japanese, *Satori.*

    The Christian, *The Kingdom of Heaven.*

None of these can give enlightenment. For the actual experience of enlightenment is enlightment, and each individual has to find it in himself. No one can do it for him and no teaching can guarantee to give it to him. The above are merely pointers to help along the way.

Ultimately the whole human race must realise enlightenment if it is to survive. Anyone can get it if they want it. No doubt some cataclysmic event will be required to shock everyone in to it. Yet there is no guarantee.

Except that Life is eternal and will always be.

As the great Hindu epic, The Bhagavad Gita has it:-

*That which is has always been; that which is not has never been.*

Finally, enlightenment is a state of supreme transcendent bliss that can only be experienced, never explained. Once experienced all else is dross.

---

*The Kingdom of Heaven is within you.*

# Book 3

# MORE THOUGHTS ON ENLIGHTENMENT

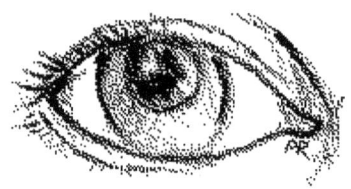

What is the meaning of Life?

There is no meaning: Life is full of meaning.

The meaning is that which is between two statements. (By the word meaning is understood that which is the 'mean' or that which stands between — 'stands under' — two ideas, things, statements, feelings etc.).

The two contradictory, or paradoxical, statements give rise to a new emergent which is the meaning, and which is both and yet neither.

What this new emergent is in itself can only be felt, be experienced. It is ineffable, beyond words, inexpressible. And when it is so experienced it is — for want of a word — called 'enlightenment' and all is joy and wonder.

To experience this state is the purpose of life. All life is joy but this state is the optimum joy. Life strives continually to reach this state.

But what is life?

Can I tell you? Can you tell me? Can anyone tell you? No. Yet everyone knows what life is. That is, if they are alive. If they are not alive they are not aware of anything.

Perhaps here is a clue.

To be alive is to be aware.

To be aware of what?

To be aware of one's own being.

So one can say life is simply to be aware of one's own being.

To be alive is to be. Life is being. Being is life.

But what is being?

Being is a verb. Being is that which stands between the two nouns, birth and death

Being is movement

---

I have been puzzled by the idea of enlightenment for years. Have I been working towards it? Yes, I suppose I have, no, I know I have. But what is it? What is enlightenment? Well, all the relevant authorities on the matter say no one can say what it is, it is something that is ineffable, beyond definition. You only know what it is if you have it. (This makes it sound like a thing, something you can see and grasp.) But, of course, the whole point is that it is not a thing, it is that which is beyond the concept of a defined thing or object.

There seem to be two aspects to it, two ways of experiencing it. Firstly, the sudden realisation of ultimate reality which comes upon one with no warning like a thunderclap. This is a feeling, a sensation, that overwhelms one with such intensity, such a combined joy and sorrow that you feel you can only hold it for a second yet you want it to last for ever. It seems to tear you apart yet enlarges you simultaneously. You are at once nothing, a mere speck in a vast impersonal ocean, and yet the ocean itself, a drop of water yet all the water. This sensation surely is enlightenment. The overriding sensation is one of Love, an all embracing love that encompasses the whole cosmos and everything and every one in it. This is why it is combined joy and sorrow: joy for the beauty and wonder of all life and creation, sorrow for all the suffering that is seen to be necessary to it. It is Absolute Love. One knows why 'Jesus wept' Can you stay in this state continuously? Plotinus, the Greek Neo-Platonist, is said to have experienced it four times.

Then there is the second aspect. One talks of someone being an enlightened being. Traditions of all cultures describe the search for enlightenment and the gradual working towards it. But what does it mean to work towards it? You may work all your life and never 'get it' The 'getting it' is simply having the experience mentioned above. And the work is to prepare oneself so as to be able to have the experience. Yet in some mysterious way you cannot make it come, it comes as an act of grace from the supreme intelligence of all life or, as some would say, it comes from God. Zen tradition talks of the student working away meditating for maybe years hoping to have the sudden thunderclap flash which makes him an enlightened being. (The koan method of Zen is one method hoping to produce this.) After the student has reached this state he returns to society as a normal human being once more and no one notices any difference. But is he the same? Has the experience changed him?

Yes it has, profoundly. He is, in essence, no longer the same being. He moves and acts at all times from a feeling of Love. (By Love I mean Eugene Halliday's definition, which is the best one I know – 'Love is the will to work to develop the potentiality of all beings'.) Also there is Augustine's, although it is dangerous unless properly understood, 'Love and do what you will'

There seem to be many degrees of enlightenment depending on the individual concerned, and I am sure the potentiality for it is in everyone and almost everyone has at some time in their life had at least the merest glimpse of it (Eugene Halliday says on page 1 of 'Reflexive Self Consciousness' – of which more later – 'these powers man must either attain or perish from the earth as unfit for the next necessary step in the evolution of consciousness'.)

Who has not experienced a sudden heart stopping moment at seeing some splendid sunset, or on witnessing, on a sunny day after rain, a rainbow arch across the sky? William James in his book 'Varieties of Religious Experience' calls the sudden rise of such feelings 'Peak Experiences', others call them 'Aesthetic Experiences'. Many people also have this feeling of sheer awe and breathtaking wonder at looking at some magnificent Renaissance masterpiece in a museum. All these are simple forms of enlightenment. Others of a far more intense degree occur in cases of extreme bereavement or acute danger. Captain Joshua Slocum, on the first solo yacht journey around the world, in a situation of dire peril felt the presence of the pilot of the Pinta (one of Columbus's ships) alongside him and guiding him to safety.

Even more powerful are the experiences of the ancient prophets and medieval saints and visionaries — Elijah being 'caught up to heaven' — John in Revelation 'I was in the Spirit on the Lord's day and heard behind me a great voice as of a trumpet' — Thomas Aquinas who after his vision said 'All my writings are as straw' and never wrote another word — Saint Teresa of Avila — John of the Cross — and many others 'in the Spirit' as they normally expressed it.

Have I ever had such feelings? Well, apart from what I may call the usual momentary experiences of sunsets, rainbows, great paintings, music etc., there have been four occasions of much deeper import.

The first was as a boy of 10, when I stood in the garden and looked up at the dark night sky pricked out with a myriad winking lights, all seeming to speak to me. An earth shattering thought suddenly thundered into my head and heart 'Why is there a world? Surely the obvious thing is there to be nothing, not something'. I stood rigid for I don't know how long, unable to move, as this weird sensation of the strangeness of existence swirled around in my boyish brain. Eventually I was called back into the house but the experience haunted me for years, and as I see now, set me on my life's course.

The second occasion was as a young man wandering into the Fitzwilliam museum in Cambridge. At the end of an aisle I saw a gigantic statue of a naked man with a club. I recognised Hercules. I went up close and stood in awe at the huge figure towering over me. With some hesitation I touched one of his feet. Immediately the oddest sensation swept through me. I felt his living blood course through me, linking him to me. The continuity of the ages ran through as a living thread from him to me. I knew his being. There was no time, there was only the present. I can give no adequate explanation of the sensation except that it had the most profound effect on me. I have never forgotten this experience.

The third occasion came at sea. Among other of life's activities I became an ocean yachtsman and had many minor experiences of sheer terror and equally sheer beauty which often gave me 'peak experiences' of varying degrees of intensity. The one I speak of was of much greater import. In company with two crew members I was delivering a wealthy business man's yacht from Palma, Majorca in the Balearics in the Mediterranean to Corpus Christie in Texas. We had crossed the Atlantic, stopped briefly at Antigua, then on across the Caribbean and were now on the last leg, sailing in the Gulf of Mexico. Here we experienced a Northerly Buster, a common fierce wind in that area. It was the morning after the storm and I was alone on watch, my two companions asleep down below, steering the deeply reefed yacht, which required a deal of effort and concentration as the seas were enormous, slowly dying down but still able to deliver a lethal kick. There was no margin for error and my senses were highly tuned. It was a magnificent morning, with a splendid sun, a clear blue sky and a sharp crisp dying wind. The sun ran across the wave tops with their dazzling white crests and caught the water droplets in thousands of tiny rainbows. Oh, I cried aloud at the unutterable beauty and grandeur and majesty of the scene! I sat, unconsciously steering, totally spellbound. How could anyone live and see such power? What did life matter? I had seen such beauty – let me die now – nothing after this had value! How long I was in this exalted state I do not know – subsequently I blessed the fact I was an experienced seaman and sailed the yacht well and did not let my sleeping friends down, yet I sailed with no thought of so doing – maybe half an hour, but during this time feelings passed through me of such power I thought my frame would give and I would die. I wanted to die. Yet I was so full of joy. Slowly I returned to normal and all was well again. But since then I have never been afraid of death. I'm sure these experiences could be far better described: all I can say is there seem to be no adequate words that get anywhere near providing someone with a full picture of what sweeps through one and lifts one up, it just is impossible.

As for the fourth experience I will come to that later. First, let's get back to Eugene Halliday and his book 'Reflexive Self Consciousness'. This short book of just over fifty pages is, I think, Eugene's greatest work – (possibly 'Contributions from a Potential Corpse' just beats it). It is, as David Mahlowe says in the preface, 'the seed-kernel of all Eugene Halliday's teachings'. It sets out to describe what Eugene calls a 'state of transcendent self-awareness', what it is and how to attain it. He further says, as I mentioned earlier, men must either attain this state or perish as unfit for the next evolutionary step of mankind. He further says that 'So important is this for human evolution and the attainment of freedom and the power to produce an adequate response in every conceivable situation that if its full import were grasped , the whole effort of humanity would be directed towards its attainment'.

Phew! A staggering thought!

I'm not here going into the detail of the book (it can be obtained online and in bookshops – see www.melchisedecpress.net) except to say that Eugene in his usual fashion first defines the terms he intends to use and then proceeds to explain the nature of consciousness, both normal and transcendent, and how the attainment of the latter confers perfect freedom, a state of which the average person who thinks, erroneously, he has it anyway has no true notion.

It is a marvellous book and I have read it I don't know how many times. As a lifelong reader over a long lifetime I know of no book, so short and so dense in its argument yet told with such clarity that equals it. In it Eugene was clearly writing for future generations. (He said once 'My day will come'.) I foresee it, like the New Testament, annotated and numbered according to paragraphs so future scholars and students and academics can quickly refer to any part of it – and argue like the Scholastics of old over the placing of the odd comma! – seriously, I foresee it in the coming age becoming an official textbook. I'm sure Eugene was aware of that. A great and seminal work.

And yet for me I missed a certain and vital 'something'. When I first read it I recognised its immense importance. For years afterwards I kept saying to myself 'I must get Resec – (Eugene's abbreviation of

Reflexive Self-Consciousness) – before I die. It's essential. Everything must give way to that'. And, of course, I was always failing. I never seemed to get any nearer. In my stupidity I thought of it as a kind of course of study which if I would diligently pursue I would eventually be rewarded with the degree of worthiness and henceforth I would be a being endowed with a transcendent state of self awareness. I kept thinking, 'I'm not there yet, but keep working and one day I will reach the goal'. ('Oh, what fools these mortals be!' says Puck in The Midsummer Night's Dream.) I didn't yet truly know what the goal was. What actually was a state of transcendent self awareness? I unconsciously felt it had something to do with the type of experience, the 'peak experience' I have just described. But nowhere in Resec is this apparent. Eugene seems to be describing the Resec state in an intellectual way, there is no mention, nothing, of the timeless joy and sense of wonderment, the marvellous and miraculous sense of peace and harmony and sheer delight at just being alive, also the overwhelming sense of power allied to utter humility, that I had experienced and knew in my bones to be true.

Why is this? Maybe I know the reason. Eugene himself must have experienced these feelings, in fact lived continuously doing so, yet he deliberately excluded any reference to them for he was writing for students to study and actuate, and we live in a secular world of science where only rational and scientific principles can gain credence. As I said, he was writing as much for the future as for the present and any mention of mystical and spiritual feelings would have negated his claim to be taken seriously. Though, of course, in other places he writes extensively of spiritual matters, in fact never ceases to do so, but here, I feel, he was writing, what I may call, an official text book on the subject in order for it to be studied in the light of the modern scientific approach which requires a Classical, a solidly rational, impersonal and empirical eye, with no hint of the Romantic and starry eyed. He was writing to be read in a hundred years time. We live in the coming age of Aquarius, which will last for just over 2,000 years. Every age is a new era and brings with it a powerful new Mindshift, which is a progressive development from the previous one and which takes the full extent of the age to come to maturity before giving way to the next mindshift. Thus does evolution proceed. The Aquarian age will go beyond the present paradigm with its emphasis on science and ever increasing technological development and pick up, and unite with, previous ages' more spiritual predilections. The Classical and Romantic modes of apprehending reality will merge. (Though there is no guarantee: the human spirit, with its freedom to pursue its own course, may choose otherwise.) Eugene obviously knew all this far better than me, he was writing to prepare the ground, for it would take probably centuries for the two modes of thinking to come together. Though already there are many signs of its nascent approach Eugene concentrated on the near future not the far distant. But I think it a pity that, notwithstanding his marvellously clear explanation of how to get Resec one gets no clear vision of what it *feels* like when one has it.

Of course, one cannot live continuously in the three heightened states I have described, they are far too intense. In those states one passes beyond one's personal being and for that short period — (the intensity of which depends on the power of the particular vision) — becomes one with the universe and its spirit. If you stayed in that state you would merge with it and 'not come back'. I am sure that has happened in some cases. But once the state has been experienced it is always remembered, in fact one longs for it to return, and it sinks into the background of one's consciousness and governs all one's future actions. This last state is the one I think Eugene is writing about. He says that 'To gain resec a certain simple exercise must be practised, in principle continuously, in early practice probably intermittently'. The exercise involves saying to oneself when one is, (Eugene's words) 'looking at something, or considering an idea or experience, a feeling or emotion, or performing any action, one must say to oneself, 'It is the Self which is consciousness itself which is looking at this thing (or considering this idea, etc.). This Self I am. I return to the Self'.

Of course this Self, which is the consciousness, or sentience, of the Infinite Eternal Spirit, God, who is all empowering and all embracing, is replicated. in the individual and tiny self. It is the same Sentience writ small. The infinite Self uses the finite self to express itself, realise itself, manifest itself. In the resec experience the self reunites itself with the Self and thus experiences the dualism of being nothing while at the same time being everything. It, for that moment, 'stands between' the two states. It is the 'mean', the meaning of them.

And this state is overpowering, it is total joy and total sadness, and one is full of laughter and full of tears at the same time, for one has overcome them both. Eugene's exercise helps one get to this state, but one doesn't say the exercise to oneself continuously for eventually one is in the state continuously but on a, can one say, reduced level where it is, as I said, in the background of one's consciousness and thus governs all one's actions. It is written 'God is Love'. This is metaphorically, spiritually and literally true. When you live in the Resec state, the Enlightened state, you live in a state of Love, love for all of life, and because you can't, as a tiny individual in a vast world, love everyone, you love all those who come within your orbit – though Jesus managed it and died for it. To become enlightened you have to first awaken from your normal so called waking state which is really a sleeping state. Most normal folk are asleep most of their lives. But a moment can come, no one knows when or how, or if it comes at all, when one suddenly questions everything. It can be a sudden bereavement, a shock of some kind, an emotional crisis which evolves into a spiritual crisis, a sudden thought which appears out of nowhere in one's mind and which can change one's life for ever. This 'Awakening' is usually the result of some period of crisis in the mind, which crisis is termed theologically 'The Dark Night of the Soul'. When the dark night comes to its end it is followed by the most marvellous and ineffable Awakening which then governs one's life henceforth. One is then 'Reborn', which Jesus talks of all the time as the prerequisite for entering the Kingdom of Heaven The Reborn state is often referred to as being 'Converted'. Saints often write of the moment of their conversion which they remember with great clarity. When this happens it is often accompanied by a call from God to undertake some worthy task, which often involves hardship and some danger, but so imperative is the call they do not hesitate, being prepared to give up their lives if necessary. The reason why so many people refuse the Reborn state is because they instinctively know it means giving up their normal self-centred life and surrendering themselves to something far greater. To be reborn you have to give yourself up to God, be prepared to do his work no matter what it takes, and this requires courage, one must take a huge leap into the unknown. And, as I say, this leap can come suddenly out of the blue or it may take many years to slowly develop and mature and then actuate miraculously at some unknown and unforeseen moment. But when that moment comes there is the most liberating feeling you have ever known and will probably never experience again at that intensity. Henceforth you are a changed person. No wonder Eugene said if humanity realised its tremendous import its whole effort would be directed towards its realisation.

Now to my fourth experience which was the most profound and soul changing of all. In one sense it was commonplace for it involved a simple affair with a woman, in another sense it was anything but, for it was in no way carnal — I never even kissed her — it was entirely spiritual. It lasted three years and at the end I was no longer the same person. (Though my family whom I see every day never noticed any difference.) The woman was a sailing friend and one day we went for a walk along the cliffs near her home. She idly said to me, 'I love it here. Will you bury my ashes here when I die?' (She was twelve years younger than me.) I replied, joking, 'Of course, if you'll do the same with my ashes too'. Later, I was looking over a couple of photos of her sitting atop those same cliffs. She had the most wonderful dimpled smile and her eyes shone out with, to me, absolute love. As I gazed more deeply, the thunderbolt struck. I was speechless for I don't know how long. Later I wrote a sonnet about it and gave it to her which she gratefully accepted and later said she thought it very good.

This set in motion a three year train of events during which I wrote almost weekly, sixty Love Sonnets, each of which I gave her as finished and which she smilingly accepted. She never verbally acknowledged them and I knew she was, at a deeper level, untouched by them. She was thus to me a catalyst, tearing me apart before rebuilding me anew, while still remaining completely and unaffectedly herself. For the love sonnets were not simple expressions of my unrequited love for her, although in a shallower sense they were that, but on a deeper level they were expressions of my love for the 'eternal feminine', for all of life, for my opening awareness of my love of God or, as Eugene would say, for the 'Absolute Sentient Power'. However, for me, this somewhat abstract idea of the 'A.S.P.' became centred in a particular woman and through her I poured out my love, from the particular to the universal and cosmic. Put simply, she became my Muse. She was Beatrice to my Dante, Laura to my Petrarch. She was my Isis, my White Goddess.  Let me quote here from the dedicatory poem of Robert Graves to his book called The White Goddess.

> Green sap of Spring in the young wood a-stir
> Will celebrate the Mountain Mother,
> And every song-bird shout awhile for her:
> But I am gifted, even in November
> .....
> I forget cruelty and past betrayal,
> Careless of where the next bright bolt may fall.

It is an age old story, experienced by others a million times over, but when experienced in oneself no less mind shattering.  Of course, I was aware of this in a semi conscious way as the sonnets unfolded, and when looking at them now I see the bi-fold meaning behind many of the lines  They were, in many ways, at once particular and universal.

As I said, the whole experience lasted three years, during which I lived a completely normal unnoticed life, while at the same time inwardly undergoing torments of utmost anguish, an experience I have described as 'exquisite pain'.  I was being ripped to shreds yet it was marvellous.  It was the strangest and most ambivalent of feelings.  I longed for, yet dreaded, it to last for ever.  Slowly, very slowly, it began to die down and eventually went altogether, but leaving a residue which has lasted ever since.  I became possessed by a surge of creative energy and activity which has gone on these past twenty years and shows no sign of diminishing.

I am now 88 years of age.

Is all of this enlightenment?  You must judge.  All I know is. I am at peace, both with myself and with the world.  I have come home.

---

Sonnets Of Love I privately published as a little booklet.

# Book 4

# PARADOX

> Jesus said to them; When you make the two one, and when you make the inner as the outer and the outer as the inner and the above as below, and when you make the male and the female into a single one, so that the male will not be male and the female not be female ....... then shall you enter the Kingdom.
>
> Gospel of Thomas: 22

What is paradox. What does the word mean. It comes from two Greek words, *para* and *dox*. The first means beside, the second means opinion  The dictionary gives two meanings: 1) — contrary or beyond opinion : 2) — a self contradictory statement that may be true, as in *to be cruel to be kind*.

This second meaning is the one usually understood as paradox. There are many statements in circulation to illustrate this meaning, as: *This statement is false — You can save money by spending it — I can resist anything but temptation* (Oscar Wilde) *— A wise fool — The beginning of the end — All animals are equal but some are more equal* *than others* (Animal Farm, George Orwell). There are many others. Make your own list.

The one I wish to speak of here is of the something and the nothing.

When I am out sailing the deep ocean and have been out of sight of land for several days, sometimes a strange feeling sweeps through me. It is an instance of what William James in his book 'Varieties of Religious Experience' calls a *peak experience.* Most people have at odd times had various forms of this feeling which can range from just a sudden light headedness to the extent of a loss of consciousness. It often comes on being deeply moved by a piece of music, on witnessing a splendid sunset, on reaching the summit of a difficult mountain climb, of falling in love and so on. It is a wonderful, liberating, exhilarating feeling and if experienced with any great intensity, never forgotten

At sea my feelings have ranged from the slightest to the most intense. When the last, a shudder runs through my whole being such that I feel my frame will break. It can last from a few seconds to perhaps half an hour. The ocean extends beyond me in a vast limitless circle, in the centre of which I am, a mere dot. I am a tiny drop of water in a boundless expense of water. I am nothing. Yet I am not nothing. I am all things. I am greater than I was.

I am a tiny nothing and I am a huge something. This is the paradox. It is impossible to describe this feeling of being in these two states at once. It is beyond ordinary living, it is beyond time and space. You feel joy so great you can embrace the whole world: you feel sadness so great your tears will never cease. You feel these both as one all encompassing feeling.

'Oh, Lord, give me words to express my joy in sadness. How can I give justice to your love.'

Only by being that love yourself.

What precisely is this feeling. How make a start at describing it. For I know I am on the edge of just touching the hem of the seamless garment of ultimate reality which is ever beyond my reach. I know that ultimate reality is all things and is yet nothing. I know that ultimate reality is full of meaning and yet has no meaning.

What is meaning.

Meaning is that which stands between two statements. Meaning is the *mean* between them.

What is the meaning of, say, goodness. To explain it you have to bring in its opposite, evil. The two imply each other, are mutually defining. And the meaning is that which lies between. Yet this does not imply a duality. For that which lies between the two conditions is also above and beyond them, it contains them as modalities of itself. So it is a unity, not two. Here is the paradox.

The Hindu Sanscrit expresses this in the word *advaita* which is usually translated as *not one, yet not two,* itself a paradoxical statement.

When I experience this I experience the two states, being a mere dot and being all powerful simultaneously. They are both and yet they are neither. I am a mere spark, which is of no import: I am a vast burning fire. I am a clod of earth, I am a cosmos of infinite intelligence. The experience transcends both sensations, it is ineffable, cannot be adequately described. It is something new, something outside the ken of the man in the street. Yet every man in the street has it in them to experience it if they but open themselves up to it.

In fact all scriptures, sacred writings and texts, all calls from the prophets, mystics, holy men, saints, all point to and express the urgent need for salvation, which is precisely this experiencing these two modes of being simultaneously. Jesus, in the Gospel of Thomas says 'When you make the two one and the one two then shall you know the kingdom of heaven'.

Eugene Halliday, my mentor, calls this state Reflexive Self-Consciousness, which for convenience sake he abbreviates to Resec. He says in his book of that title (page 28) 'So important is this for human evolution and the attainment of freedom and the power to produce an adequate response in every conceivable situation, that if its full import were grasped, the whole effort of humanity would be directed towards its attainment.

'When you make the two one and the one two'. When you make the something nothing and the nothing something. That is the task. What exactly is this nothing, what this something.. And how bring them together.. This is the supreme paradox. To understand this is to know the ultimate reality and the meaning of existence.

---

The something and the nothing are one and the same, the first being just a modality of the second., the whole making up what is termed ultimate reality. In other words the something comes from the nothing, is just a mode, just an activity, of the nothing, just a thing, a form, which, so to speak, *grows as a seed* from the non thing, the formless. This formless, considered before it exists as form, we call God, Allah, Brahman, Tao etc. When it has become form we call it Creation, the Universe, the World etc. And the two exist as one, just as in the human being Consciousness exists as one with the Body. (For consciousness is the nothing, as the body is the something.)

The nothing is God as he is in himself before creation: the something is God as he is in his creation. The two interpenetrate each other and make for life.

All life, all existence expresses itself in three modes, passive, active and a third neutralising force which balances the two. Another way of expressing it is 1) free, 2) bound and 3) freedom = (freedome, the balance of the two). The ancients called these *Jupiter* = (Deus Pater, God the father), *Saturn* = (Satan), *Mercury* = Hermes, Thoth, the Messenger, the Messiah.

The normal way of understanding the meaning of life, and particularly in this modern secular material age, is to regard the material world we see all around us, this visible universe, as the real world, as the only world. But if we do this we are seeing only one mode of existence. We are seeing only the active mode, the Saturn – Satan – mode. This is the world of form, of structure, this is the world of things. But there is another world, an invisible world that was there before the visible world came into existence. This invisible world produces the visible world. This world is formless, is free, is Jupiter, is God.

Shakespeare's king Lear says, 'Speak again. Nothing can come of nothing.' He was wrong. Something *can* come from nothing. A thing can come from nothing for the nothing (no-thing) contains the thing hidden in itself as a potentiality not yet activated, as a seed waiting to burst forth.

The actual nature of what this nothing is, which is not a thing and yet has a thing, a seed, hidden within it is the great mystery. The actual nature of God as he is to himself is incomprehensible to the human mind, for the human mind is a thing and to understand a no-thing (nothing) you have to be a nothing and nothing can understand nothing. In this sense Lear was right. But nothing in this case is God and somehow God just simply *is* in a way beyond our comprehension. The only way we can understand God is to become God. In certain circumstances it is possible to get an inkling of how God feels to himself, for although the mind is a thing, consciousness, as I previously stated, is not a thing. No one has ever seen consciousness, it is that in which things are seen. So consciousness, which actually is a spark of God, can grasp a fraction of the nature of God, for you are God acting in the place in which you are. If everyone acted according to this there would be no more wars.

I said, in certain circumstances. What are these circumstances. This is the third mode, the neutralising force Mercury. Mercury is the Messiah, who is the Saviour. Salvation consists of the balancing of the nothing with the something, of the interpenetrating of the two.

From the formless springs form. And this form initially is just a dead shell or husk until the formless – another word for which is *spirit* – breathes it into life. 'And God breathed into it the spirit of life.'

By experiencing this visible world we see around us and in which we live as the only real world, we are only half alive. Gurdjieff, the Armenian sage and teacher, says ordinary man is asleep all his life, and he spent many years teaching men how to wake up and to reach the state he calls *self-remembering*. This is identical to Eugene's Resec.

One needs to get oneself into the position of being balanced between the two states of being. One needs to sit on the fence. (A much misunderstood phrase.) In the negative sense it means being indecisive, not being able to make up one's mind. It means being lukewarm, being indifferent, not caring. In the positive sense it means living on a knife edge, perfectly poised and balanced between the two states of life and death — (for that is what they are) — and thus supremely sharp and alert and ready to leap off the fence, on the instant and on the correct side, knowing it will be the appropriate side for the situation. In this situation you are fully alive and every cell in your body trembles and thrills through and through with vibrant life. (On a joking note Eugene used to say that for this reason he always slept on the edge of the bed.)

This is the state of my experience when out deep ocean. I can die at any instant and I thrill with radiant life. I am in Resec.

But how to reach this state? What must you do? Why does no one do it? Why has hardly any one heard of it..

Firstly, hardly anyone knows of it because it is in the interest of those who rule the world to keep the population under control by ensuring it plays no part in the world's education systems, and also because most of these rulers are ignorant of it themselves. But if you do hear of it, usually by being told of it by someone who *knows* – and there are many of these unsung heroes about – then once your eyes have been opened, you see evidence of it all around. The universe takes on a wholly new aspect. The world's sacred texts are full of it.

Secondly, how do you reach this state of Resec, of self knowledge, of self realisation, of true freedom. Begin by just believing it is true. Then just prefer it to all else. Just by doing this you find things begin to happen, apparently inexplicable things, all leading you forward. You may say, you can't do it, it all sounds far too way out and difficult. Don't be put off. Just believe it, just *prefer* it to all else. This simple act of preferring is sufficient to set the process in motion and you are on your way to returning to your true origin, to finding your soul, to becoming who you truly are. Of course the way is long and hard and will take over your life, but you will find that life has become immeasurably richer and once experienced you will never return to your previous and mostly unsatisfactory life.

Thirdly, why does no one do it. Simply because the price is too high. For the price is that ultimately you must die to your creaturely self, your ego self, the self you normally call your real and only self in order to become you true self, your soul. Believers think you *have* a soul. This is not true. You *are* a soul. A soul living in a physical body. Your true self is your soul. This soul is the Immanent Spirit of theology, which is one with the Transcendent Spirit which is and who is God. When you become one with your true self, your soul, you become a little god, you become God acting in the place in which you are. This is a dangerous doctrine unless properly understood. (Many fanatics go about killing people saying they are god.) This is why it is not taught at large. In the ancient mystery schools and in all the world's religions, all those seeking spiritual enlightenment had first to undergo a period known as Purification to prove themselves fit to receive the teaching. They had to become 'as a little child', innocent, without guile, humble, totally trustworthy. 'Blessed are the pure in heart for they shall see God'. (Matt. 5:8)

Apart from the instant *metanoia* – conversion – it normally takes a long time, sometimes lifelong, to reach the state of total surrender to the Infinite Spirit who is the Ultimate Reality. It's all very well to simply say, 'Just prefer it to all else, that is all that is required'. When first told of Resec, the individual self immediately recoils, for it instantly senses deep in its innermost depths that it will ultimately lead to its own death. This is a mistaken notion, for it does not mean you cease to exist as a being, but that your normal self that up till then has lived for itself alone, now lives in a world that is as before but now includes everyone else as well. It is a much larger world and you are a much larger being.

If one is determined to get Resec one usually approaches it gradually, taking it easily, not straining or getting stressed when nothing seems to work or to happen. One just keeps one's consciousness firmly fixed on the goal, letting it happen or not happen, knowing with utmost certainty that in the fullness of time one will succeed. One simply *Lets go, let God.* Have faith, he will see you through. And he will. There is all eternity. Yet one must beware of complacency. Remember Saint Augustine's 'Dear God, make me perfect, but not yet'.

And then, on a certain day, the call will come and you will hear your inner voice saying 'Surrender yourself to me. Surrender yourself to God. The time has come.' You will feel your flesh shrink in fear as it takes in the full consequence of such a deed. But you know in your heart the moment of truth has finally arrived. It is now or never. Can you do it. If you refuse, how many lifetimes will it take before you are ready once more? You remember the poet's cry :

'Deny Love not — it may not come again.'

You must make the leap over the edge. You must internally say, and truly mean it, 'Dear Lord, I surrender myself to you. Take me. Your will is my will. I have no will of my own except it is also yours. What would you have me do? Into your hands I commend my spirit.' Something along these lines you must verbalise to yourself. Then just let go. Throw yourself off the cliff edge, not knowing if you will survive the fall. Can you do it. It takes courage.

For sooner or later you will have to do it.

When you do you feel an immediate release. The die has been cast. You have done it. You can do no more.

Then you find nothing has happened. The world goes on as before. No one notices any change.

But change there is. It is like the change of the tide. I live by an estuary and I have observed it many times. The tide comes creeping in from the open Atlantic ocean beyond. For three hours it moves up the ever narrowing river into the closing hinterland of people and cities, increasing in speed and power as it does so, until it reaches its zenith — high tide — after which for three hours it slowly decreases until it imperceptibly appears to stop altogether and it is low water. Slack water has arrived. All is still, there is no movement. You watch fascinated. Then a tiny movement, the faintest ripple, merely a suggestion of a change of direction. Yes. It is there, the water is flowing, only just, but it is definitely flowing back and outward to the expanses of the great ocean. At the end of three hours it is in full spate, speeding on its never ending rhythm of ebb and flow. If you are out in a small sailing vessel at this time,, and if the wind happens to be coming from the opposite direction — wind over tide, as the saying is — you must, as another saying has it — when the sea horse jumps, look to your pumps.

But, seriously, this nautical analogy is an exact description of when you make the decision. You have made a *metanoia*, you have made the change, and just as the tide turns, so it is with you. At first you feel nothing except the wonderful sensation of release. You are in slack water, a period of rest before the new flow in the opposite direction. 'Go with the flow.' For it will lead you out increasingly into the open ocean and true freedom.

' For what shall it profit a man, if he shall gain the whole world, and lose his own soul.' (Mark 8:36)

And again, in the previous verse 'For whosoever will save his life shall lose it'.

---

Here is the ultimate paradox, the paradox that transcends all

# Book 5

# JANUS

I wear around my neck a silver charm, talisman, symbol, call it what you will, which is an image of Janus the Roman god of doors, a double-headed, laurel-wreathed figure facing both ways, away from the old, ahead to the new. One cannot walk into a new room without walking out of the old. Janus also represents the turn of the year. The old year dies as the new is born. It is a truly universal symbol with many meanings and connotations and is eminently suitable as a subject for meditation. I have worn the image round my neck for over thirty years as a constant mnemonic of its, at least for me, most potent meaning. This is of the inner and the outer. Jesus said – Gospel of Thomas – *When you make the two one, and when you make the inner as the outer and the outer as the inner —— then shall you enter the kingdom.* So what does this mean? What is the inner and the outer?

The outer is the external world, the material world, the world of the senses, the world most of us recognise as the real world and the only world. The inner is the world behind this, a non material world which is the causer of the outer material world. Most people don't recognise or give credence to this other world. But in order to get a true picture of ultimate reality both worlds need to be kept continually in mind. Hence my silver Janus.

The inner world causes the outer, or rather they both exist simultaneously. But before the outer came into being there existed that which caused it, namely the inner and this is the only true reality. The outer can be considered as an illusion for it is actually a reflection of the inner, on which it is totally dependent. The external world can be likened to a beautifully engineered automobile. Behind this superb artefact lies the designer in whose mind the automobile had to exist as an idea before it could come into existence. No designer, no automobile. Every action you perform exists first as an intent in your will, then as an idea, and only lastly does the action come forth The action is observable, but who has ever seen an intent? Clearly the intent is the more significant as it controls the type of action. If the intent is true and whole then the action is necessarily so also. So it behoves always to be able to control the intent, which requires first being aware of it. Most peoples' intents are unconscious and so they continually produce actions, the consequences of which put them, or others, in harm's way. Hence the need to know the inner as well as, if not more so, than the outer.

But how do you know the inner? The external visible world seems to most people to be the only world. They include in this their own body and they think their body is all that they are. Their sense of identity becomes located in their mind, which governs all they think and feel and do. The mind is that in you which gives you your sense of separateness. You become identified with your name and form. However, deep within you is a deeper self, a truer self, which ultimately is one with all the other selves. All life is one. The life in the mineral, the plant, the animal is one with your life, for there is only one life but which yet manifests in the myriad forms in the universe. Your self is one with the Self of all selves. This One Self is your inner self, your 'still small voice' which you can only hear when you silence the incessant chatter of the external world and of the world of your computer-like mind which is never switched off. It is the Immanent Spirit, which is one with the Transcendent Spirit.

All beings seek Freedom. The requirement for attaining it is to bring the inner into the outer and the outer into the inner. 'Make the two one' as Jesus said. Everyone is aware of the outer, but few are aware of the inner. People, nations, rush about crying out for Freedom, arguing, making wars, setting up protest movements, demonstrating, yet they never achieve true freedom. To do that you must first put your own house in order. 'Before you cast out the plank in your brother's eye, first cast out the beam in your own.' If people first sorted out their own internal problems – Know Yourself – before attempting to sort out other peoples' and the worlds' then there would be fewer conflicts and wars in the world.

What is Freedom? Most people would say it is, 'Being free to do what you want'. But if that is so, are you free to determine your wants? Want is a strange word. Want, Wont. Want implies a lack, something you lack, something you need. But, surely, if you are free you do not lack, you do not want anything. And Wont. That implies something you habitually do, customarily do. 'I do such-and-such for that is my wont.' But if you are free, you do not customarily do something, you are able to do anything. It seems Freedom is a much misunderstood word. I would say Freedom is being able to do what you will, not what you want. Saint Augustine said, 'Love and do what you will'. That's a bit better. Eugene Halliday said 'Freedom is the ability to choose your own bondage'. If these two statements are true, freedom seems to have something to do with love and bondage. Bondage. But isn't that what freedom means you have now cast off? And will. We could alter the statements to 'Freedom is the ability to will your own bondage'. We are now in a paradox, an apparent contradiction in terms. Freedom is willing your own bondage!

So where do we go from here? And what has this to do with the inner and the outer? Well, it's partially explained in the very word 'Freedom', which can be split into two, namely 'Free' and 'Dom'(e),

Free Dome. And there is your paradox. A 'Free' which is 'Domed' (i.e. imprisoned) and a 'Dome' which is 'Free' (i.e. let out of prison). The Free is the Inner and the Dome is the outer. If you can bring these two together in your every willed thought, feeling, and action then you have Freedom.

Okay, so we know what is the outer, for that is the external world, the material world, the world of your body and of your senses. Then what exactly is this inner world, this non material world? Is it not exactly that, the non-material world? One could say, the inner world is nothing and the outer world is something. When the two come together you have freedom. Actually, of course, they are never apart. They are inextricably intertwined. The very concept of the something implies its opposite, the nothing. Then how describe this nothing, how define it? Well, it cannot be defined, for to define is to limit and the nothing is limitless. The nothing is not a thing, that is, it is not a substance, not a circumscribed object as is the something, the external world. Yet it somehow 'is'. If one has to say what in essence it is, the best one can say is that it is 'awareness', an intelligence aware of itself. Yet this awareness is nothing, that is it is not a formed object that you can see, measure and evaluate. To say truth, you find this awareness expressing itself as your own consciousness, your own awareness of yourself. And you have never seen your own consciousness as you can see your body. You just take it for granted. Freedom consists in being able to be aware of the nothing at the same time as you are aware of the something, of being able to listen to your 'still small voice' at the same time as you listen to the chatter of your physical voice and the world outside, of being aware of your consciousness at the same time as that consciousness is aware of its actions. Achieving this state is usually called being 'Enlightened'. being 'self-realised'. Eugene Halliday's term for it is 'Reflexive Self Consciousness' which he abbreviated to 'Resec'. Resec is the highest evolutionary state of being available to man, beyond which are other higher states as yet beyond us. Resec has been realised by few humans as yet, but we are approaching a time in world evolution, in fact we are almost there, when resec will start to be achievable by large sections of the world's population. For this is the coming age of Aquarius, when humanity will ultimately be unified, become one, when for most people the inner will be as the outer.

How is it possible, you may ask, to be aware of the inner and the outer at the same time, to be aware of your consciousness at the same time as that consciousness is being aware of all your thoughts, feelings and actions, is in fact the agent governing those motions? If you are creating a work of art your whole consciousness is involved in that process. You cannot at the same time be evaluating and criticising the work you are doing, for while you are doing that you are no longer creating. The two processes are incompatible. What actually happens is that the two processes are vibrating so rapidly from one to the other that for practicable purposes they appear as one process.

All great artists have Resec. Take Shakespeare. When he creates, a sentence or even a whole scene, flashes into his consciousness apparently from nowhere. This 'nowhere' is the nothing, which is yet the source of all things, the ultimate creative power of the universe. It is the indescribable, the indefinable fount of all wisdom. It is the place from where come all great discoveries, all intuitions, all inventions. Shakespeare has no control over when or where these flashes of insight come, as do none of the great poets, scientists, philosophers and other thinkers who have given so much to the human race. They come whither they will and unannounced. 'The spirit blows where it lists.'

Shakespeare's own critical faculties now come into `play` - excuse the pun - and he, as he writes, evaluates, modifies and improves what he has received from the higher source. The two processes, the creative and the critical, are fundamentally incompatible. You cannot create while you are criticising, nor while you are criticising can you create. But the great artist can move so rapidly between the two they appear to be the one process. That is Resec.

If you try this in your daily life, what you do is this. As you have an idea, experience a feeling, or perform an action, at the same moment you do these things you also observe yourself doing them. If you hit a ball, for instance, as you hit it you observe yourself, as if from the outside, hitting it. You may say this will affect your efficiency in hitting the ball. Well said. Actually it is impossible to do the two things exactly at the same time. Your attention as you hit the ball. if it is to be effective, must be fully engaged in that operation, but a fraction of a second afterwards your attention then returns to yourself. You 'reflex' your consciousness back upon itself. If you don't do this you will become fully identified with the hitting of the ball to the loss of your own unique centre. And the retaining of this centre, under all conditions and in all possible situations, is the true meaning of freedom. Without this, you are simply a slave to the ball hitting or whatever other action, feeling, thought, possesses you. The ordinary person gets pulled into, is identified, with what he does to the extent that he forgets himself. Thus he becomes a slave to it. He is a slave to his feelings and emotions, his ideas, his thoughts, his actions. The resec man, on the other hand, never forgets himself, for at the very moment of identification he pulls back and returns to himself, to his consciousness, which is not a finite form. He returns to the 'nothing', which is yet a full plenum and is his essential self. Thus he brings the inner and the outer together as one. He does not deny the outer external world, he lives in it just as before. It is the same world but he sees it differently. He sees it, every aspect of it, as a glorious sunlit expression of a supreme and loving intelligent power and he is one with that power. For he is a free man in the real meaning of that term. 'Love and do what you will.'

---

# Book 6

# BEING

'To Be, or not to Be'                    Hamlet

I lose to find.                    I die to live.

Our birth is but a sleep and a forgetting:
The Soul that rises with us, our life's Star,
Hath elsewhere had its setting
And cometh from afar:
Not in entire forgetfulness,
And not in utter nakedness,
But trailing clouds of glory do we come
From God, who is our home:
Heaven lies about us in our infancy!

Shades of the prison house begin to close
Upon the growing Boy,
But he beholds the light, and whence it flows,

He sees it in his joy;
The Youth, who daily farther from the east
Must travel, still is Nature's Priest,
And by the vision splendid
Is on his way attended;
At length the Man perceives it die away,
And fade into the light of common day.

.....

Thanks to the human heart by which we live,
Thanks to its tenderness, its joys, and fears,
To me the meanest flower that blows can give
Thoughts that do often lie too deep for tears.

Extract. 'Ode: Intimations of Immortality'<br>William Wordsworth.

---

What follows are two short pieces. The second was written over sixty years ago, during the 1950`s, when I was in my twenties. I came across it while clearing out a cupboard. It is a monologue which I performed several times at a friend`s house where he had monthly gatherings. Reading it again after all these years I detect a connection between the two pieces. Interesting to find such a continuity running through one's long life, and how one's defining ideas are present from, can one say, almost from birth.

---

I am floating in a limitless ocean. It spreads all around me and I sense no bounding horizon. Then I sense it is all below me as well. Am I drowning? But, no, for it is all above me, too. Am I in the air? The water and the air, the ocean and the sky seem to be one with nothing to separate them. Where am I? Am I anywhere? Am I everywhere? Am I dead?

No, for I feel life flowing through me more intensely than anything I've known. This, whatever it is, I am floating in has a strange light permeating it. Have you ever seen, on a dark moonless night at sea, the wake of the ship streaming astern and lit up with phosphorescence? That is a very dim image of this light. Phosphorescence is a living light for it is made up of millions of tiny organisms. This light was like that. The whole unbounded sea-sky I was floating in was a living light, a strange and unearthly and heatless purplish light. It seemed to be glowing and yet it wasn't. It seemed to be a kind of darkness and yet it wasn't. And I was one of the tiny organisms making up this living light. I could feel the living light darkly shining through me as I could sense it all around me. It was in me and I was in it. I felt totally alone. I was the only one in the universe, there was no one else. Yet there was no fear, no terror, only a beautiful sensation of being in my rightful place, of having come home. I cannot describe the peace, I cannot describe the love sweeping through me. I could rest here forever.

And I did. Or so it seemed to be. For time did not exist. Do you know that feeling when you wake up after a good night's rest? You find you have been asleep for eight hours or maybe more and yet it feels like only a minute or two between falling asleep and waking up. You have felt nothing of the time between and you know something happened during those eight hours of which you have no memory and yet which has fully refreshed you. This feeling was something like that except I remained fully awake the while. I was – how can I say? – I was asleep and yet I was awake. I truly wish I could describe the sensation. I knew nothing, yet I knew everything, I was an utter fool, I was a sage, and all these words, these terms, mean nothing, are meaningless. There was just a limitless wholeness, a limitless sphere or globe of living light of which I was the centre and of which I was the circumference also.

Then I realised I was not alone. Although I could see nothing yet I could feel and I felt myriads of living sparks in this living light of which I was at once part and of which I was the whole. And the sparks, the spirits, were all love, as I was all love. How long I remained in this state I do not know, a minute, a thousand years? No matter. It was all one.

Then came a gradual darkening and a gradual falling. And I slowly began to awaken but now in a different form from my previous wakefulness. Memory began to go and a new memory began to form and strange yearnings swept through me. Of what these yearnings were I do not know, they were just very powerful yearnings for something, I know not what. The darkening and the falling continued and slowly increased and then gradually ceased and I was still And I was alone, the living spirits had gone and I was isolated and suspended in nothing. Then came an abrupt and sudden sensation of falling an immense distance, as of a parachutist whose chute has failed to open and then I hit the ground and I was nothing.

An aeon passed and then I saw, or rather felt, a series of visions which were of a world in which I was, and this world was as nothing I had known and yet was strangely familiar, and I lived in this world doing things I had never done before and yet were also strangely familiar. Was I reliving some past life? Was I living in a life to come? I did not know. I had no past, I had no future. The images ceased and I found myself once again in water.

Only this time it was a different kind of water, real water. Whereas the first had been a — I have no words — a celestial, an ethereal water, that which I was now in was comforting and warm and I slept in it for what seemed ages. All memory, both previous and subsequent, had gone and I was again nothing, a nothing floating in nothing — no — floating in water.

Gradually life began to return. I moved. I wriggled. And I felt constriction. The constriction became more and more and I was in a tunnel, which gradually closed in until it was a mere pinprick and through which I had to go. There was pain. Oh, such terrible pain, increasing and increasing! If it continued increasing like this I knew I would die. Yet it did continue. I knew that soon I would have to let go, surrender to the pain. Every so often the pain went away. Then it returned with increased strength. The tightening all around bound me, pressed me in upon myself with such excruciating pain that I fought it and I fought it, but at last I knew I could bear it no longer and — I let go. I totally surrendered. I abandoned myself to whatever was to be. I gave myself to total nothingness. Darkness closed in. And I died.

---

There was a sudden release. A bursting. A flooding in of light I began to breathe. There was a cry. Then a voice.

'You have a boy! A lovely baby boy!'

There was laughter. And I felt a soft warm pair of globes pressing close and I saw a pair of laughing eyes full of love gazing down upon me.

I was born.

---

## A Christmas Monologue

DARKNESS    A LONG SILENCE    THEN A VOICE.

In the beginning is the word.
Which word is this that you hear now.
Before the word, out there in the silence, in the darkness,
You waited – passive, quiet and expectant
You were nothing – not yet an audience –
For 'Audio' is 'I hear', and how can you hear
When nothing has been spoken?
And I was nothing also, for I had not yet spoken.
Now I have spoken and I am become something;
I am become a speaker.
And you now can hear, and have also become something;
You have become an audience.
When the nothing becomes something,
That is called a birth.

The very first birth of all came also with a word,
Which word was – 'Let there be light'.

### THE LIGHTS COME ON

This birth was, and is, a very strange thing, and hard to speak of.
In the darkness, before there is any birth,
When there is only nothing, and therefore no thing,
From where does that word come that brings the light
That makes us start with joy,
And rejoice at the birth of the blazing orb of day,
Heaven's brightness, the Sun?

If the word is the birth,
Then what gives birth
To the word?

How does that word arise?
From where does it come?
And how?  And why?


We speak with words – we communicate with words –
But how can we speak about that which *was*
Before words were?
Words cannot speak about the wordless,
For the wordless is silent,
Even as the sunless is dark.
And where is there communication
If there is silence?
Or light if there is dark?
And also, where is there life
If there is silence?
If there is sunless dark?
For a birth, which is the beginning of life,
Begins with a spark,
Begins with a cry.


A word is a thing,
And *before* the word,
There *is* no thing, and therefore
Nothing.


Before the beginning, therefore, before the word,
There was ―――――
Nothing.
And we cannot speak of it.
All we can say is, 'Before the word there is ―――'
And then stop speaking.


We *express* nothing and so make no *impression*.


And so it was before the beginning,

Before the word,
Before that first great cosmic birth,
Before the sun gave forth its light.


What there was just sat there, passive, quiet, and expectant,
Like a woman waiting, dreaming,
As you the audience were before this speaking started.
What there was, was nothing ———
A No Thing.
Yet with everything inside it, latent and potential,
A woman, a womb, a mother of all living,
Waiting for expression, waiting to make its own *im*pression.
And it waited: and it waited: and it waited.
For someone, something,
To make the first move.
Waiting for something to happen.
And the waiting became a yearning and a hunger,
A yearning of the nothing for the something.
A yearning as of a woman for a man,
A womb, a void, aching to be filled.


And still it waited –
For someone, something,
To make the first move.
But there was no one, there was no thing.
There was nothing other than it.
It was alone.
And as it realised this –
As it felt its aloneness —
It trembled —
*It trembled.*

And this trembling was the beginning of the birth.

For this trembling was the first move.
The first move had been made.
By itself.  Upon itself.

Did it tremble with excitement?
Did it tremble with fear?
It trembled.


And the wheel began to turn.


Only began, for it was not yet a wheel,
For a wheel is that which goes right round
And comes back on itself;
The movement first was forward; forward with excitement
As it realised it was alone and could do as it willed,
For there was no one to stop it.
But as it realised this it started back with fear
As it felt its utter, utter aloneness.
And this backward movement completed the circle,
As of a serpent catching its own tail in its mouth;
And it became a wheel.
And a wheel is a will,
And this wheel, or will, began to turn.


Out of the nothing had come something,
And the something that had come was a will,
And the will was the will of the nothing
For the something.
But once it had begun to become something
It tried to run back in fear to the womb
That was the nothing.
So it is as if there are two wills;
The will of the nothing to become something
And the will of the something to return again
To the comfort of the nothing.
It is as if there are two wills
And yet there is only one will,
Pushing against itself,
A vicious circle,
A back and forth movement,

An out and in,
A pulsing;
And this pulsing movement is the trembling,
And this trembling is the beginning of the birth.


The spin of the wheel, once begun, accelerates,
Neither will can satisfy itself.
The will of the nothing for the something
Is not satisfied, for it cannot drive forth
In its hunger for experience:
It is imprisoned in the wheel.
And the will of the something for the nothing
Is also not satisfied, for it cannot sink back
Into the deep sleep from which it came:
It, too, is imprisoned in the wheel.
The will is held in a prison of its own making.
To be held in is to be in hell.
The will is in hell.


And the spin of the wheel, or the will,
Grows faster and faster as it struggles frantically
To free itself, and it begins to darken
With the speed of its spinning,
And begins to become an object.
An object is an orb ejected,
A something thrown out from the nothing,
As a woman puts forth a child.


And so the birth continues.


The pain and the anguish of the imprisoned will
Increases and increases and increases,
And the pressure inside the wheel builds
Up and up and up,
And then ———
Suddenly and without warning ———

The will ——
Stops struggling
And lets go —— it lets go.
It surrenders itself up entirely to its fate.
It dies to itself
The pressure is all of a sudden taken off,
And the wheel, the will, the object,
Becomes incandescent,
And it lights up.


And the sun is born.


For heaven is equilibrated power,
Opposing forces perfectly balancing each other
So that each is no longer itself but the other.


The will is in heaven and the Sun is born.
There it hangs in the sky,
Glowing, shining, resplendent.
So also is the Word born,
Out of the dark womb of the Nothing,
A heaven-balanced will to illuminate,
Like an orb in cloudless noon,
A seeing Eye and a speaking I.
The only begotten Son of the Father.
And the Father loves the Son as himself,
For it is himself, as its Mother is himself.


And the Son, who is the Father, is speaking the first word,
And the word is
'Let there be light'.
And his saying it causes it to be so.
And the fact it is so enables him to say it.

The Nothing, who is the Father, who is no thing,
Has become something:
He has become his Son.
And now for the first time
We can speak of him,
For his Son is the Word,
And with words we can speak,
And we can call the Son the Son,
And that which caused the Nothing, like a womb,
To give birth to the Son, we can call the Father.

In the beginning is the Word.
And the Word is the Son of the Father,
And the Son and the Father are one.

And everything that is,
Comes to be in this same Way,
Through this same door of Creation,
This one and only Truth.

Let us rejoice at the birth of the Son.

Amen

MUSIC

———————————

# Book 7

## A WAY OF LIFE

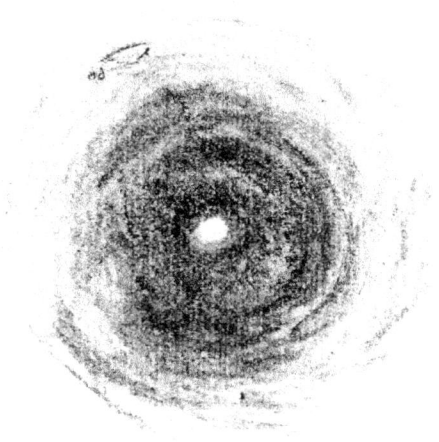

Seek the still centre. Once found, stay there.

Awake ! O, Pilgrim, Awake !
Set your foot upon the Road
That stretches ever upwards
— Do not look back —
Until at last, ever narrowing.
Is reached the summit, where
The path becomes a point, a centre,
The navel of the world, and here
The Universal Soul resides,
And you have found your *soul*.
For you and He—She—It are One
And now you know yourself.
No more the toil and suffering
Of the world, for here is Love
And Peace and Harmony.
And back into the world you
Can return, and spread that
Marvellous Trinity into the
Hungry, thirsting people,
For you and Love are One
And you can henceforth Serve.

Awake ! O, Pilgrim, Awake !

Philip Rose

When I say our life is a journey, my daughter smiles and says, 'I don't agree. I am not on a journey. I just live my life, I do my best, and then I die and that's the end. There is no journey.'

Well. of course, there is a lot of truth in that. But is she right. Let us see.

---

As we move ever closer into the $21^{st}$ century – and the age of Aquarius, of which more later – a sickness of increasing proportions can be seen in the so called 'developed' Western world. I do not speak of the many wars that are everywhere breaking out or are in an advanced state, for there have always been wars of greater or lesser degree ever since man became a thinking being. No, I speak of the 'information age' in which we are now living. With the rise of the radio, television and particularly the internet and social media we in the West, and increasingly in the whole world, are bombarded with news and information of every kind from the trivial to the profound every second of the day and night. It is all too much to take in, the poor human brain reels under the onslaught and longs for a bit of silence. Mental breakdowns are now commonplace and suicides, especially among the young are spreading at an ever faster rate. A general sense of unease, of any sense of purpose, pervades society. No one knows what to believe, no one trusts authority or anything or anyone or anything. Society is slowly but surely breaking down. The population senses the ultimate approach of anarchy and chaos. The strident rousing chorus from the musical 'Hair' 'Now is the dawning of the age of Aquarius', rather than a positive, takes on the negative and sinister note of a descent into the cacophony and inane blare of mere meaningless noise.

The disharmony seen everywhere in the external world is replicated in the internal world of the lone and isolated human soul. No one knows who they are any more, just as no one knows what society is, what civilisation is, what the world is anymore. The world has no purpose, life has no purpose, they have no purpose. No wonder the number of suicides. Everything is breaking down.

What can be done.

Many self-help books are now being written, many courses are now being offered, all telling us how to live a full and satisfying life, how to be at peace with ourselves and the world, how to overcome worry and stress and so forth. All part of the information bombardment they themselves seek to alleviate.

Can the church, can religion help.

The Western world, by and large, is a secular world. My granddaughter and her husband, both in their thirties, are professed atheists. Many of the political and business and corporate institutions operate on an atheistic basis. Science is the new religion. Mention the world religion to the average westerner and he straightway thinks you are referring to the teachings of the church and he thus is at variance with you.

But religion, or at least religion as I understand it, does not mean the church. Certainly the church has over the centuries been the custodian of the religious teachings, but it has so distorted those teachings that now they are no longer accepted by the majority and so religion itself is no longer accepted

But religion is not the church.

The word religion, apart from its usual meaning of 'to fear God' means also to tie, to bind, from the Latin 'ligare'. Re-ligare thus means to bind back or rebind. In the past religion held society together, people lived with religion every day of their lives, religion gave a common purpose to the meaning of life. Yet as society evolved and we reached the Renaissance and the rise of the Scientific spirit doubts crept in. Men and women began to think for themselves and no longer accepted the distorted teachings of the church. (They were distorted because they were understood literally, not symbolically and allegorically.) During the $20^{th}$ century people no longer believed God created the world in six days for now it is accepted that a day is more than a mere 24 hour period. It is a general term for a period or division of time. (Eastern teachings which go back thousands of years speak of the Day and Night of Brahma, both of which are understood to last for millions of years.) The idea that the Bible is to be understood in four ways, literally, symbolically, allegorically and ontologically is only just beginning to be accepted. So the church has gradually over the last two centuries lost its hold and now has very few adherents.

But the people long for the sense of security and certainty that the church once provided so they now feel lost and turn in their desperation to material things and consumerism. The TV seems to consist in large part of food programmes. Comfort fare. Also most of the books and courses previously mentioned are superficial and simply pander to the material aspect of people's lives — how to enjoy life, be happy, how to succeed in business, be popular, succeed in love etc, none of which truly answer to the people's deeper and more spiritual needs.

Spiritual needs. Now we are coming to it. For that is the only thing which fully and truly answers the problem. That is what will bring harmony where now is disharmony. Spiritual. A dirty word these days. Only a brave man – or a wise fool — dares to utter such a word in polite company now.

Spiritual. What does this 'dirty' word mean. It comes – as always – from the Latin 'spirare' to breathe. The ancients said the spirit was the wind, the breath, that something which is invisible but yet that which causes life.

Shakespeare's King Lear, carrying the dead Cordelia in his arms, cries :

> She's gone for ever!
> I know when one is dead and when one lives;
> She's dead as earth. Lend me a looking glass;
> If that her breath will mist or stain the stone,
> Why, then she lives.
> This feather stirs; she lives. If it be so
> It is a chance which does redeem all sorrows
> That ever I have felt.
> And my poor fool is hanged. No, no, no life.
> Why should a dog, a horse, a rat have life
> And thou no breath at all. Thou'lt come no more
> Never, never, never, never, never.

Pray you, undo this button; thank you sir.

(To see this play and hear these lines near the end, especially that last line, can break the heart.)

The spirit is vital. Without it we are nothing. The ancients taught that man is a threefold being composed of spirit, soul, body. (The human can be classified in various ways from one – original unity – right up to seven but this threefold one is the most important.) The human is said to come from spirit (the breath or wind 'which blows where it lists' and is the origin of all phenomena and life itself) and is an immortal soul encased or imprisoned in a body. The human does not *have* a soul, it *is* a soul. This soul has a body. As thus it can orientate itself either towards the spirit or the body. As so:

$$\text{spirit} \leftarrow \text{soul} \rightarrow \text{body}$$

What it usually does is orientate itself mainly to the body to the extent of identifying itself almost completely with that body while being barely aware of its spiritual aspect. The human soul is actually the Spirit (God the Infinite Intelligence which is formless but the source of all form and is all pervasive) acting in the place where the soul is. If the soul knows this it is in perfect harmony with itself and with all creatures and with all creation for it knows that all is one and from one source. And if it knows this it has solved its problem of uncertainty and stress and anxiety. Its troubles are over and it can now live in the 'peace which passes all understanding' and can also live to its optimum level, developing its talents and thus making a contribution, however minute, to the common good and to the evolutionary process.

You are God acting in the place where you are. Let us examine this strange and startling thought more deeply and clearly for it contains the answer to all mankind's problems.

Firstly, unless properly understood, it is obviously a very dangerous doctrine. Imagine some madman or terrorist, as many are indeed currently doing, calmly going about shooting or bombing people at random thinking he is God or is doing God's will. The Yorkshire Ripper killed 13 prostitutes saying he heard God's voice telling him to do it.

There is an Eastern story which goes: A man went to a teacher and asked him about God. The teacher said 'God is everywhere and is in everything'. Satisfied the man went away. Going along the road he saw an elephant coming towards him with the mahout riding on it. He thought 'God is everywhere and in everything, God is in the elephant, God is in me, can God harm God. I will walk straight on'. When he got a little nearer the mahout asked him to get out of the way. But he said, 'No, God is in the elephant, God is in me, I am going on'. When he reached the elephant it simply took him in its trunk and threw him into the hedge. The man, shaken and bruised, limped back to the teacher and said 'I have been trying to do what you said and look what happened'. The teacher replied, 'You fool. It's true God is in everything. God is in you, God is in the elephant, but God is also in the mahout and the mahout told you to get out of the way. You disobeyed God and got what you deserved'.

This doctrine that God is everywhere and is in everything has been known from prehistoric times, but because of its dangerous implications if not properly understood has always been kept secret from the mass of people and only revealed to the initiate who underwent a long and rigorous training in the Mystery schools of those times and pledged on pain of death never to reveal it to the profane. Jesus was an initiate and taught in two ways, one to the populace and another to the disciples. (And the disciples came and said to him, 'Why speakest thou unto them in parables.' He answered and said unto them 'Because it is given unto you to know the mysteries of the kingdom of heaven but to them it is not given' Matt. 13:10-11) Yet he hinted at it openly. ('The kingdom of heaven is within you', 'I and my Father are one', and further, Jesus answered them 'Is it not written in your law, I said ye are gods.' John 11:34.)

When seen like this it is all so simple. Yet no one sees it. Why is this so. You are there already, you are perfect and at peace with yourself and all and everything. You don't have to do anything, you don't have to work at becoming 'saved' or becoming a 'realised' being, becoming very learned and wise. You are already there. All you need to do is realise it.

Ah, now here is the rub. Why do so few realise it. It is as if they are living in a house of darkness. Outside the sun is shining in a cloudless sky on a splendid landscape of rich beauty, of mountains and valleys, of rivers and sea and luxuriant foliage and all kinds of animals all at peace with one another. You don't see this for your windows are covered in all kinds of detrita which are your self-absorbed and individual aims, desires, loves, hates, false ideas and simple ignorance. You see only the shadow of the real world. So, yes, you have to do something. First, clean your window. Tidy the house. Sweep away all the clutter. Plato describes this in his famous Myth of the Cave. A group of people live in a cave and spend their time watching shadows on the wall in front of them – T.V. – while behind them shines light. Eventually one of them goes to seek the source of the light and climbs up and out of the cave. He sees the world outside, sun in full splendour, and the people walking about, laughing, happy, playing and conversing in joyous abandon. He goes back into the cave and tells his companions to come up and outside as he's found the real world and they are only looking at the shadows being cast. The others ignore him and continue studying the shadows.

But, you may say, 'I don't see shadows, I see the world in which I live and it is wonderful. I go to work in the day, I go to sleep at night, I have my family whom I love, I have my friends. That is life. What more does a person want. I don't understand what you are saying.

Yes, how can one disagree with that. But is it enough. Be honest with yourself. Have you never wanted anything more. I do not speak of wanting more money, of wanting to succeed, of wanting fame and so on. Lying in the dark in bed at night, does not some degree of unknown yearning come and disturb you and you try in desperation to push it away for you see it as hopeless Why am I here. What is life. Why do I have to struggle so. What is the point. It's all meaningless.

I suppose such thoughts only come at a certain age when you have been exposed to the vicissitudes of life long enough. When you are young life is different.

When all the world is young, lad,
And all the trees are green,
And every goose a swan, lad,
And every lass a queen;
Then hey for boot and horse, lad,
And round the world away,
Young blood must have its course, lad,
And every dog his day.

Charles Kingsley

Ah, those were the days. Yet the young still have their own problems, mainly one of finding their own identity. If you do not have these thoughts and yearnings then I am not for you. If you do then I am.

The ancients said that the first stage in finding harmony is 'The Awakening'. You must awake to the feeling that all is not right and if possible something needs to change to make life bearable and significant. Most people never awaken in this way and never feel the need for change, or if they do, feel nothing can be done about it. So they just accept life as it is, though deep down in their innermost depths they know it is not and should not be so. But if you feel these faint stirrings of awakening rising to the surface that will not be stilled, what can you do?

Well, these faint stirrings are enough. They will set you on the path if you go along with them. Don't at first do anything. Just live your life as usual, but keep firm in your faith that you are beginning to awaken and something can be done. You will begin to notice a subtle change occurring. You will start to notice things which you previously took for granted take on a different perspective. Strange coincidences will appear. At the very time you had been wrestling with some problem you will idly come across an old book on a bookstall which answers the problem. Or you will hear, while working in the kitchen a sentence on the radio which does the same. You think of an old friend you hadn't seen for years, 'Yes, he would know' and then in the street you will meet him. Odd things like this will start to happen. Jung called them synchronicities. You are beginning to feel a strange force, a benevolent force, which seems to be helping you. This is the power of the universal force which has created the universe and is the universe and is in you and which is helping you for you are helping it. How are you helping it? By beginning to realise you are not a single being in a hostile universe making your way in spite of all the other beings. For that is how the majority of humankind sees itself. Each human is at war with his neighbours and struggling to make good in spite of them.

As it is with each individual so it is with mankind in general. Here neighbour struggles with neighbour, here society fights society, here nation fights nation, hence global wars. Only here and there, dotted among the mass of humankind are the few individuals following a different path, a different way of life.

What is this different way of life.

It is the way of Love. Love of life, love of all things, of all creatures, of all beings. My mentor, Eugene Halliday, gave the best definition of Love I know which is quite different and much more profound than that generally understood. He said 'Love is the will to work for the development of all beings everywhere'. Just think on that and its implications for a moment.

The faint stirrings of awakening I mentioned are the first stirrings of this Love.

This love will grow as time goes on. It is a positive force for good that will flood your whole being, and your blood will circulate more freely through your system, your thinking will become clearer, and your actions more geared to helping your loved ones and all with whom you have contact. In short, you are beginning to grow more at one with the whole universe and its wonders and less involved with your own – now seen to be – petty problems. You will marvel at it at first and have doubts it is anything more than a coincidence that you find yourself waking up more bright eyed and looking forward to the day than usual. But if you keep firm in your faith and belief in your having preferred to change rather than having placidly acquiesced in the 'status quo' then the love within you will steadily grow. Remember, this love has always been within you. Whatever private guilts you may have or evil thoughts and deeds you have done, this love has always been there. All you have done is release it. You have made the choice. You have reached the point in your life when you have realised there is a choice and you have made it and it is the right one. This choice, which everyone has to make sooner or later, is whether you are on the side of universal life or on the side of yourself, on the side of your own private purposes. Or, put another way, to become on the side of God or the Devil. The Devil. What are you talking about. What has the Devil to do with it. Let me explain

The Devil is the other side of God. (Oddly enough, the word devil is 'lived' backwards.) As universal purpose is God, so private purpose is the devil. God leads ultimately to eternal life, the Devil to limited life and ultimately to death. Put another way, Life is wholeness, Death is partiality (partiality is private purpose). The whole is always greater than the part.

Are you for the whole or the part, i.e. your separate part. That is the choice. Christ said, 'No man can serve two masters'. Either you are for God or Mammon. What do I mean by 'private purpose'. When you live for yourself alone, when you see yourself as a separate being in a world of separate beings all ultimately striving for survival.

'I don't see myself that way', you may say. 'Certainly. I am a separate being but I'm not at war with my fellow beings. I do my best to live alongside them and co-operate with them as and when the need arises.'

But do you. When your aims clash, do you not retaliate. Are you never angry. Do you never feel resentment. Do you never feel envy at your friend's success and your apparent failure. Are you fully at one with yourself. Do you never get stressed when you are obstructed in your purposes. Can you truthfully say all is at it should be.

I said earlier that the first signs of 'Awakening' are when you feel the first stirrings that they are not. I said these stirrings will set you on the path and to just live your life as usual and you will find it subtly changing. One of the changes is you begin to become sensitive to your own inadequacies and to start to do something about them. You will want to take yourself more in hand. You will find yourself saying, 'I was angry with my wife just now. Why. It was my fault. No, it was no one's fault. It's all wasted energy. Stop being angry. But I can't help myself, I just get angry. Very well, next time I am angry I'll not try to stop it, I'll just let it happen and just watch it like a disinterested observer'. You will find doing this subtly changes the anger and it will disappear. What has happened is that the energy of the anger has become the energy of watching the anger.

For all is energy. There is nothing that is not energy. Energy is all. The whole universe, and whatever it was that created the universe is simply energy acting in various ways, in different modes. That which created the universe, which is intelligent, formless, invisible and beyond any naming, and yet has been called many names of which the one we use is 'God' is this energy. God is pure energy creating the universe, and the universe is this energy formed into its many modes. (The atom is the tiniest of forms and when it is split a vast amount of energy is released.)

The universe can be said to be God's body, while God himself as he is in himself is invisible within it. Just as you, in your body, have you as you are in yourself, your awareness of yourself invisible within it. God is awareness of himself: you are awareness of yourself. God is energy: you are energy. God is macrocosm: you are microcosm.

*Become who you truly are.* For this is the way of life.

And the Aquarian Age I spoke of earlier is the beginning of a process which will last for a little over two thousand years and take many centuries to come to fruition and which will culminate in the whole human race living this way of life.

What is this Aquarian Age.

It is part of a cosmological process called the Precession of the Equinoxes lasting for 25,920 – call it 26,000 – years and describing a complete circling of the heavens, which the ancients named the Zodiac, and in which the earth occupies in succession each of the twelve segments or signs of the Zodiac for 2,160 years. The whole process is called the Great Year and the process through each sign is called a Platonic Month. Each sign or age produces a significant change in the evolutionary movement, each age comes in with various earth changes and what the ancients called 'strange perturbations'. The change comes in gradually, like a change of tide, reaches its zenith and then passes out slowly to the beginning of the next sign.

Scientists are unable to precisely determine when Aquarius comes in and the previous sign of Pisces passes out. Some say it will take hundreds of years. Others say they think the change over occupies a time span of roughly 80 years from about 1960 to 2040. If the latter, there are certainly weird things going on as of now (2016). And note the date of 1960, the start of the 'permissive age', of youth, of sexual freedom and in fact all forms of freedom and individualism. (Though these are not true freedoms for that is another matter.) Strange things are indeed afoot. Not to mention climate change. No one can dispute that the world at present is in a peculiar state of ferment and of 'strange perturbations'.

'This is the dawning of the Age of Aquarius' and it will last for just over 2,000 years. What will it bring.

No one knows, of course, and predictions into the future are hardly ever correct. 'There is always the unexpected 'as the saying goes'. All we have to go on are present events and past events and what we know of evolutionary processes. We can follow the past ages and see how they proceed in a consistent pattern to a recognisable end. To follow this pattern out fully would take a whole book. Suffice to say that it moves steadily from a state of unity towards a state of diversity, or perhaps it would be better to say a state of unity–in–diversity. Owen Barfield says that early man existed in what he called a state of 'Original Participation' in which he felt himself not as a separate being but as part of the world he saw around him. He was a spirit and everywhere was spirit; spirit in the flowing water, in the whispering trees, in the motionless rocks, in the tiny lizard on those rocks. Everything was spirit and everything was one. Everywhere was vibrant and radiant and 'the morning stars sang for joy'. 'If the sun and moon should doubt they'd immediately go out' as Blake says. It was the golden age. Everything was God.

Slowly this unity faded as man grew more and more separated from his environment, his fellow men and from creation. (This is a necessary phase in the evolutionary process.) Unity waned as diversity waxed. Psychic awareness waned as individualism and rationalism waxed. Eventually psychic awareness disappeared almost entirely as rationalism took over almost entirely. Barfield called this the 'Separation' period. We are now existing in the prime of this period. Barfield then called the third stage 'Final Participation'. This is when the rational mind finally rediscovers its lost psychic past and proceeds to live with both faculties working together in harmony and hand in hand with each other. (We are beginning to see the first glimmerings of this in the changing fortunes of male and female, where each is slowly beginning to become the other while still retaining their original orientation. This will ultimately lead to the birth of the true androgyne.)

I believe this Aquarian Age we are coming into now is the slow genesis of this 'Final Participation'. Mankind, notwithstanding the terrible events going on in the world at present, is on the road to becoming a fully integrated being. Where heart and head work in perfect correspondence one with the other. Pascal's famous saying 'Le Coeur a ses raisons que la raison ne connaît point' – 'The heart has its reasons which reason knows not of' – will no longer apply. This will be the new golden age. In the first golden age man was in paradise but did not know it: in the forthcoming age man will be in paradise but will know it.

This, I feel certain, is the inevitable outcome of what we are seeing now. How long will it take to reach fruition. It is beyond predicting. World events seem to be heading inexorably towards total annihilation, Armageddon only a spit away. Yet who comes in first, the tortoise or the hare. We must hope it is the first.

We must also remember – where is God in all this. If God is in everything and he is everywhere, he will only let the world come to an end when he decides it will end. And we do not know when he will make that decision.

What we do know is that life proceeds in cycles and that life is eternal. Hindu tradition talks of life as an eternal continuum which has no beginning and no end:, endless cycles of existence lasting for millions upon millions of years. They are called The Day of Brahma (Manvantara) and the Night of Brahma (Pralaya). God wakes, then sleeps, then wakes again then sleeps again and so on infinitely. Just as we do, though in a different time scale, yet in relative terms the same.

Also remember each cycle always completes its revolution before passing on to the next, which is actually the same cycle but on the next stage of evolution. In the cycle in which we are now living — and in life everything goes by threes — we are only just entering the third phase, Final Participation. And even then the world will not end but will simply pass onto its next cycle, slightly up the spiral of evolution.

Scientists reckon the sun will burn out in some billions of years hence and thus our solar system will come to an end. (But by then we will no doubt have moved on and be living in another more advanced star system!) That the world will end eventually is certain, but it will only be The Night of Brahma. We shall still be here for we are eternal and immortal.

How do you know all this. I hear you say.

I reply, how do you know anything. The answer, as I see it, is by experiencing it, by reading of it, or by being told of it. Well, I know of it by all three. Firstly, I was told of it by a man in whom I have total trust. Acting on his advice I read many books, sacred teachings and texts dating from far back to ancient times, all of which confirmed his teaching. And lastly I then began to experience in my daily life the truth of these teachings and studies. I found truths everywhere. Having thus experienced it I then, at least for myself, *knew* their truth. I knew that I knew. And beyond that one cannot go.

These teachings are not generally known, for they are not taught by the normal schools and so people are ignorant of them. Yet they are not hidden. They are everywhere if you merely look in a different way, if you look in different places.

Sir Isaac Newton, one of the greatest of all scientists, was also a great believer in astrology. When someone asked him why he wasted time on such superstitious nonsense he replied, 'Believe me, sir, I have studied the subject, you have not. The Greek thinker, Plato, still regarded as one of the most famous philosophers of all time, also believed in Atlantis. Why. And why is he regarded as thus deluded.

Absence of evidence is no proof of evidence of absence.

If you don't look for evidence you won't find it And to find it you must look in the right place, and the right place is everywhere. If you are open minded enough, all is grist to your mill and you will be open to any suggestion. Science is the new religion and scientists normally have preconceived ideas and are resistant to unorthodox possibilities and so they don't find it — say Atlantis — and thus say it doesn't exist.

---

However, to sum up. This writing is called A Way of Life. What, then, is this way of life. It is really simple, it is, in essence, the age old way, the way of the peasant, the labourer in the field, the way of living close to nature. Simple yet hard to do.

Become as a little child, yet be a wise child.

Take everything at face value, but expect anything to happen.

Trust everyone, but don't be surprised when let down.

See the world whole, not partially.

Be eclectic, all is grist to your mill.

Love the world and everything and everyone in it.

Believe that all is God.

Above all, Affirm. Say Yes. Stay positive.

Remember you are perfect.

Everyone has a talent. Find yours and develop it.

All the above is cliché and platitudinous. Nevertheless true.

Remember the big secret. Take it to your heart. It will transform your life.

Everything is one. There is only formless intelligent power in and behind all things, beings and phenomena. This power we call God. But he is also called Allah, Brahman, Tao and numerous other names. They mean nothing. The power is beyond them all. This power manifests itself as the universe. The universe and everything in it is God. Yet God is at the same time beyond the universe. God is consciousness, the universe is his body. You are consciousness living in your body  God is immortal: you are immortal.

Eric and Susan Hiscock, who sailed around the world three times in their yacht Wanderer, came across a saying by Arthur Ransome of Swallows and Amazon fame which they carved in the bulkhead of their yacht. (I, too, had it on the bulkhead of my yacht.) 'Grab a chance and you won't be sorry for a "might-have-been".'

A way of life. That is it.

A last thought. Eugene said:

> I rest like water in water, love in an ocean of love, in perfect transparency.

This is wisdom. This is the way to live.

*Seek the still centre. Once found, stay there.*

> Neither pursue nor flee from
> The twin-eyed stars
> That swing into your orbit
> But, like Apollo,
> Hang in the centre
> Motionless
> And let them circle you
> In silent harmony.
>
> Philip Rose

# Book 8

## SONNETS OF LOVE

Dedicated to her for whom they were written.

# A SEQUENCE OF SIXTY SONNETS

The English, or Shakespearean, sonnet form is used throughout.

Written between September 1990 and December 1993

## PROEM

### HER TO HIM
'Will you sprinkle my ashes when I die,
Above Welcombe Mouth near the cliff top's rim;
Where the sea-pink grows and the buzzards fly,
And, swooping and soaring, the seagulls skim?
Where the east wind is curling the wave crests back,
On the surf far below as it's spent on the rocks;
Where yellow gorse lines the steep valley track,
And gnarled oaks are shaped by the west wind's shocks?
Where we picked and chewed sorrel as we talked,
Pointing to badger holes low in the hedge;
Where I taught you wild flowers as we walked
Back up the steep path on the valley's edge?'

### HIM TO HER
'O, my love, I will do just that for you,
If you'll do the same with my ashes, too.'


## 2

Have I known you in another lifetime?
In former times and place have our paths crossed?
Did once your song and mine together chime?
And are the sacred notes of that song lost?
It could be so, I feel it in my heart,
For when you're there it is like coming home;
An old forgotten melody can start
Reverberating, echoing, from the tomb.
What were we then, together, when we breathed?
What were the notes of that mysterious song?
What acts of right and wrong by us bequeathed
That future, present, life we now belong?
There is no way to know, yet time will tell,
So let's, our present tune then, just play well.

### 3

Where there is love, relation's never forced,
And I ask nothing, do not seek to own.
You are yourself and follow your own course,
And you are you, and I am me — alone.
If I try to own you then I lose you,
To keep you with me I must let you go,
If I loose what bond I have upon you,
Your love for me, if any, then can grow.
My love for you is giving, never taking,
Denying you, if that's what you desire;
Accepting even if, my love forsaking,
You to another person's love aspire.
Love is work, with no thought of selfish gain,
The loved one's true well-being to attain.

### 4

Love is false if to loved it is in thrall;
True Love alone is free and has no check.
What love is that if, to the loved one's call,
He who loves come running at finger's beck?
That is the *passive* action of a slave,
Chained to the one he loves as to his lord;
But love that's true is *active* — as a wave —
Flows free — with its own motion in accord.
The wave, upon the rock, upon the sand,
Indiff'rent if they know of it or not,
Flows its life-nourishment upon the land,
Slave to none, unsubjected, self-forgot.
Yet wave upon an unseen wind relies;
True Love, an Unseen, Greater Love, All-Wise.

5

If, slackly musing on my life's array,
And all the wondrous things that I have seen,
The people I have met along my way,
And all the wondrous places I have been;
My, idling, wandering thought upon *you* falls,
The blood at once runs faster through my breast.
I wake, sit up, the idling mood then palls,
And gone, forgotten, paled is all the rest.
With senses sharpened, only then I see,
What has been all along before my eyes,
Just by the window hums a working bee,
I'm child new-born, all life is a surprise.
You are the yeast that quickens life for me,
Your presence blinds me so that I can see.

6

In later life your path converged on mine,
And henceforth I am now awake, alive.
I sprawled, old lifetime's habits on, supine,
But now my step is sprightly and I thrive.
I used to walk each day familiar roads,
Where constant use had made excitement die,
But now my new found lightness has no loads,
My step's so lissom, Puckish, that I fly.
What have you done to make me alter so?
How could I at this latter age grow young?
Why should my dying embers so new glow
That old and boring songs now seem new sung?
Yet all that you have done, and with no guile,
Is, like the sun at dawnrise, just to smile.

7

I have suffered a sea-change; or maybe
Rather, a return to younger, source-near,
Waters, ever springing from that nascent sea
That births creative, youthful, visions clear.
In those early days, when free ran the sap,
All things could be done — easy move the world!
Years of effort on, still unchanged the map;
Disillusion then, sad the flag is furled.
But now a miracle: A sea-change thrills!
In my old age the world is young again!
I can create; have refound old lost skills,
The sap runs freely through my teeming brain.
What's re-birthed me, made my eyes sparkle, shine?
Just this — the course you're sailing's converged mine.


8

I look into your lovely shining eyes,
I warmly glow from that most radiant smile;
Your face so clear, transparent, where no lies
Fall ever from your full lips to defile.
So eager, boyish, girlish, as you are,
Mature and wise, yet youthful, all in one;
Courageous, brave, no cowardice to mar;
Serious, grave, reflective, yet such fun!
All these in you I see and yet still more.
But while these attributes you so encase,
They are not yours, but come from greater store,
Of which you are the instrument and face.
The Spirit of Absolute Love shines through
That clear transparent window that is you.

9

When I say 'I love you', what do I mean?
Who is it in reality I love?
Is it just you as you, or have I seen
Reflections of a Greater Love above?
Your smile, which first I loved in you, is you;
Unique, and yet like no other smile I've known;
And yet, while you, I glimpse a broader view,
A Cosmic smile behind it and now shown.
So you are you, and yet you are not you;
A seeming paradox, so strange yet true;
For Cosmic Smile needs windows to smile through,
And when it does its smile and yours aren't two,
So, yes, I love that Greater Love, it's true,
Yet when I say 'I love you', I love *you*.


10

How can I write? My tears fall on the page;
My tears for you, my tears for him, for me.
I love you so there is no rule to gage
What length and breadth is in eternity.
Why should such joy produce such copious tears?
Are joy and sorrow always closely noosed?
It is, perhaps, that with advancing years
My heartstrings are progressive, flood-tide, loosed?
I do not know, I cannot tell, I *feel*.
And with this feeling comes this immense love,
So all embracing nothing else is real
Except these showering tear drops from above.
the pain of Love can be too great to bear;
I die of joy, and it is Heaven there.

11

I have never loved as now I love you;
I know that thus I'll never love again.
The joy of being born afresh, made new,
Is worth the price of every ounce of pain.
What matters it if you do not love me?
More to the point, what matters if you do?
Whichever way, I gladly pay the fee,
For love so deep comes only to the few.
It is a precious and a sacred thing,
So holy I profane to give it breath,
So rich that he who has it is a king,
So true that he who knows it fears no death.
You are the Beatrice to my Dante now,
Where'ere my ship sails, you are at the prow.


12

Your image has been etched upon my heart,
The lines bite sharp and deep into the plate
That is my soul, the living, beating, chart
On which is cut my fortune and my fate.
New lines that from you stem now overlay
Those weak and indecisive lines of old,
My heart is now a palimpsest to say
My life will henceforth follow some new road.
This image that thus lies upon my own,
Is perfectly composed, pure work of art,
Exampling me by line, by form, by tone,
To match each feature, imitate each part;
The more that image thus enhances mine,
The closer mine approaches the divine.

## 13

You are married to another, ah, me!
Someone you're happy with and love and trust.
I came too late to find you young and free,
To love you from afar it seems I must.
And yet, where is the hardship, sweet, in this?
Does love upon some time or place depend?
Does true love need to wait upon a kiss?
Does true love need proximity attend?
For you are in my heart and that's the truth,
And nothing, no one, can take that away;
With you so there, old age is once more youth,
My spirit soars and I'm all fire, not clay.
So if you're with another, all is well,
For as you're in my heart, it's there I dwell.


## 14

Dante saw his Beatrice one day,
In the piazza walking with a friend,
The sight was such to make him swoon away,
Her image stayed with him until life's end.
If anyone had asked him anything –
His book 'Vita Nuova' later wrote–
His answer to all questions was to sing
The one word 'Love', his single only note.
And so it is with me then, as I write;
My stock of words is now reduced to one,
This word for me's all depth, for me's all height,
For me all words now meet in union.
'Love' is this word, the only word I need,
This only in the world is worth my heed.

15

We rowed up river on that autumn morn,
Taking the dinghy to its winter rest.
The tide was neaps, two hours to flood; so borne,
We thought, the two mile row would be no text.
How wrong we were! The tide was ebbing fast,
Our progress, oh! so tantalising slow!
We made halfway, to Limers Lane, at last,
And watched the tide's so fast increasing flow.
We hauled up on the beach and tied her down,
Rested, leaned on the wall, and had a talk
Of Beatrice; how Dante's love was shown,
Then back to Bideford, with one mile walk.
What trivia! Why write such petty stuff?
Let all the world go hang! This was enough.


16

I looked out of my window to a morn
Of misty melancholy, dismal grey;
The river, sluggish leaden, flowed forlorn,
'Such Sadness' all of nature seemed to say.
The sky, a blanket slate, pressed down on all,
I heaved a sigh and felt my spirits droop.
The whole of life closed round me as a wall,
I let my head sink down, my shoulders stoop.
Then all at once across the waters winging,
Two swans swept by with powerful rush of air;
Two gleams of purest white — my heart was singing —
'Such Gladness' streamed from out the heavenly pair.
As this glorious vision coursed the sky,
In my heart's mirror I saw you and I.

## 17

The love-sick swain, what poor pathetic fool;
So serious, sighing all his life away;
Slaving himself to be his love's footstool,
Moaning and groaning if she will not stay.
Love is a game the Lord plays for his sport,
To while away his else so lonely hours,
He laughs and laughs to see the love-game fought,
To see *Her* topple *Him* from prideful towers.
Let's laugh then, you and I; go with the Lord,
Let's play his game as he would have it played,
Let each be sheath in turn, each be the sword,
Let's trip it light and not be solemn swayed.
The Lord, it's said, does love a merry heart,
Let's gladden him and play our laughing part.


## 18

In our next life I'm going to meet you young,
And woo with every art and skill of mine;
I'll polish, burnish up, my silver tongue,
Make you the subject of my every line.
That future life's too sweet to think about,
The bliss portended there is past my ken,
But that that day will dawn there is no doubt,
(Beneath Time's cloak is hidden where and when.)
They say there are twin souls that walk this globe,
I think that we are of their company,
Though they have differing role, wear different robe,
Such souls go hand in hand in harmony.
In worlds past and to come, both you and me,
Since time began, we've been, we are, we'll be.

### 19

You hold me in a sweet captivity;
Enchantress, I am yours, each ev'ry day.
If you unloosed my bonds I would not flee,
Within this cell I find me in I'll stay.
What bonds are these, though, that thus set me singing?
Is that a bondage that does so enchant?
Am I in prison if to me you're bringing
These orisons of joy that I here chant?
I love my bondage, do not seek parole,
Have never felt so free, though now most bound,
Before I was fragmented, now feel whole,
Discordant note is now harmonious sound.
So do not cease enchanting, hear my plea,
And bind me ever tighter — set me free.

### 20

In worlds past, in worlds now, in worlds to come.
We have been, we are now, and we shall be.
All kinds of places strange have been our home,
On mountains — in deep valleys — by the sea.
We've been all to each other — all relations,
You've been my sister — I have been your brother.
Husband, wife, and lovers, we've changed stations,
I've been your father — you have been my mother.
What means this interplay of parts and roles?
Is there some heart-link we may not deny?
You know there is, for we are both twin souls,
Yoked by a love-knot we may not untie.
This criss-cross changing pattern never ends,
Sometimes, perhaps, it may be we're just friends!

## 21

You have the key to my creative door,
It's now unlocked; my Muse has taken wing,
There is no height to which it cannot soar,
There is no note so sweet it cannot sing.
All worlds eternal, future, now, and past,
It traverses with such consummate ease.
With tongue unloosed, no longer an outcast,
It wills to teach, to touch the heart, to please.
Remember, though, this Muse of mine's not mine,
It's given to me by an Act of Grace;
I'm just a moon on which the sun can shine,
Its bright-eyed rays reflected in my face.
We both are blest to have been so selected,
How can such twin-love ever be rejected?


## 22

What is Love? I know *you* know what Love is;
Because you know so well I love you so,
Few there are who know, like you, what Love is;
You're Love embodied, shining with Love's glow,
You think *I* know of Love, with all my chat,
I can't begin to understand your art,
*My* love is in the head, beneath my hat,
*Your* love is where it matters, in the heart.
*Your* love is age-old wisdom, beyond speech,
Deep ocean pools of feeling, all pervading,
The love you show is far beyond my reach;
I'm on the surface, still in shallows wading.
Teach me that ageless wisdom that you know,
Those waters you swim easy – there I'd go.

## 23

When I love you, I really love myself;
But who's myself? Myself is really you.
And who are you, if you are not yourself?
What is the mystery here? Are we not two?
Well, yes we are; we are both two, yet none;
This is the paradox, the magic clue;
The Universe is Love, for Love is One,
and Love is me, and Love and I are you.
Understand it thus; there is only Love,
We both within it dwell, as fish in sea,
For nothing else exists, below, above,
And Love says, I am you and you are me.
Love loves itself, for it can love no other,
It loves itself when we love one another.


## 24

Upon this spinning globe where we abide,
There is a tiny piece of precious ground;
A little white town by the riverside,
Where I hear music of the spheres resound.
My spirit, as a seagull, swoops this place,
The sun, the stars, in ever cloudless skies;
This little white town wears a loving face,
Where every base thought that I have straight dies.
I walk on air in ever sacred street,
My heart embraces every passing soul,
I want to kiss each stone beneath my feet,
To shout that we're all part of one great whole.
My love lives in this little town, you see;
Where e'er I walk she's never far from me.

## 25

I am just a fool of Love; just Love's fool.
Love's happy wanderer in an alien land.
Eternal student in Love's boundless school,
A neophyte with ever open hand.
I am not worldly wise or slick or apt,
But simple, gullible, ingenuous;
In money matters wearing dunce's cap,
An innocent, naïve and credulous.
And yet, in spite of this, I take the prize,
I am the wisest of them all, I know.
Though fool, I have a treasure nothing buys,
More rich than anything this world can show.
This prize is Love, this treasure, love for you;
Fool's gold to some, it gilds this old world new.


## 26

There is a maid who loves the simple things,
The flashing crests of seas, the river's flow;
There is a maid who loves what each day brings,
The sun, the cloud, the mist, the rain, the snow.
She loves the dash of wind upon her cheek,
The crunch of striding feet on gravelled track;
She loves to clamber up on to hilltop peak,
To slither, laughing, down a valley's back.
She loves to be with friends, not on her own,
To wine and dine and chatter merrily.
She loves the peace within her room, alone,
When quiet imagination can run free.
My love, too, in these simple joys does dwell,
But, joy of joys, I love the maid as well.

## 27

Across the ocean's ever moving face,
The expressions of the Lord forever pass;
More ancient than time and profound than space,
They ripple and furrow this else still glass.
Instant response to every will and thought
This ever vibrant skin gives witness to;
Bodying forth and catching the uncaught,
By changing shape of wave, by altering hue.
You are yourself as this mobile ocean,
With so transparent face, expressive eyes,
Your inner love reflected in each motion
That, instant, kisses each joy as it flies.
Your face, the ocean's face, is brim with love,
A mirror of that Pure Love from above.

## 28

I wander idly in the market place,
Outside, the warm spring rain is gently falling;
'Hello!' I hear, — I turn around — your face
Is close to mine, and — whoops! — my heart is stalling.
I stutter, smile, give you the sailing book
From bric-brac stand just now for you I've bought,
You, beaming, thank me — lovely laughing look! —
I'm gauche young man again, bereft of thought.
A tiny episode, of no great instance,
Passed, spent, before a minute's time has flown,
Though trifling, straw, of no significance,
Of such small threads is Heaven's garment sewn.
Lips tender brush my cheek, then on your way,
I musing stand, and gladdened is my day.

## 29

These sonnets that I write, what is their source?
What their origin? Where their hidden home?
From what depths do they come? What is their course?
Is deep within my heart some buried tome
My love has opened, so a new light shines
On verses written, oh, so long ago
By long dead sonneteer, who penned his lines
To try, as I do now, his love to show?
How did it get there, then, this buried book?
Who was this sonneteer now born once more?
And who his love? Do I just have to look
Into his lines to see face I adore?
I do! For this past poet, he was me:
His love of long ago? Why, you are she.


## 30

Your heart is a tiny fluttering bird,
A wren in a thrusting world of hawks;
Your heart is a gentle whispering word,
In a room where the loudest speaker talks.
Sometimes your fluttering wing tip touches mine,
And then a thrilling vibrant current flows;
Sometimes your heart's shy whisper — sound so fine —
As poesy, overlays my so dull prose.
Just merest brush of feather touching feather
Is felt as thunderbolt from heaven above;
Just merest breath of whisper, altogether
Resounds as a full symphony of love.
Love has no need for size or quantity,
A whisper, feather, — there's eternity.

## 31

We have never kissed, you and I, never kissed;
Your lips and mine in love have never met.
Your lips have brushed my cheek and mine your wrist,
And that is all — no closer do we get.
Some loves there are, are fierce, full of passion,
As rockets shooting high, soon dropping down,
Each lover seeking selfish satisfaction
Of sensual pleasure solely for his own.
Some loves there are, are gentle, full of giving,
As rivers ever widening to the sea,
Each lover seeking more abundant living,
With emphasis 'for you' and not 'for me'.
This latter love for kisses has no need;
This later love is spiritual in deed.

## 32

As night's dark curtain draws across the sky,
And sun below the ocean drops from view,
A chill upon the heart can then creep by,
As sea's cold waters dim to black from blue.
The poor brave human soul feels then alone,
Needs comfort — fearful — longs for smiling face;
To phantasies and nightmares is full prone —
Mere dot in the infinity of space.
Just then high in the western sky is seen
A brilliant warming light, white as a dove;
It is the planet Venus, crystal clean,
Bathing its lovely light — the Star of Love.
Your night-dark door I've knocked on opens wide,
And, smiling, Venus welcomes me inside.

### 33

The yacht slips silent through the sleeping sea,
I sit and dream on watch, alone, at night;
The sails broad off, the wind so gentle, free;
Waters reflecting moon's pale silver light.
'In such a night' did young Lorenzo muse,
To Jessica, his loved one, hand in hand,
'In such a night can nothing ill misuse,
Or sweet and loving harmonies disband'.
The sky's star-sparkling magic patined dome,
Sea's moonlit shimmering scintillating net,
Yacht's loving cradling rhythmic roll – my home,
The heart's at perfect peace and rest – and yet.
The sky, the sea, the yacht, and I ...... all bare;
You are not there, dear love, you are not there.

### 34

Those times I, unplanned, meet you are sun's beams
Shafting so sudden, splendid, through dark cloud.
These moments when I see you! – then it seems
All life, till then so muted, sings out loud.
Most days pass by in reasonable content,
Not sad or melancholy, nor mad gay;
Most days are moderate, not straight, not bent,
Each path a gentle undulating way.
But then come moments unexpected, sudden –
The phone – I hear your voice –and my heart leaps –
You're on the slip – waiting –smile so open –
My eye, as lifting oar, with joy then weeps.
Exquisite pain, these moments not to know.
Accept, my heart! –they're Love's great ebb and flow.

## 35

I have no possessions that are not yours;
You have my heart so you have all of me.
In my soul's house, for you, there are no doors,
Ask what you will, take gladly, there's no fee.
Thus emptied so, am I to you in pawn?
Dependent on your every will and whim?
Divested, is my future then forlorn?
Am I pauper, banished to your life's rim?
Not so, for though my heart breaks every day,
As it's not mine, then what have I to lose?
The pain, the joy, I've given them all away;
Naked now, there is nothing left to choose.
I'm stripped to nothing, am nonentity;
But as I live in you, I'm in eternity.


## 36

You will never love me as I love you;
That I know so well — trustful realise.
Yet one note of your love — more than my due —
Outsings my best song — you swim in my eyes.
What you have given me, greatest gift,
Is just the simple power to feel again.
Long dead, you have raised me, made my heart lift!
What do I care if it's sun or it's rain!
I long for you to love me, long so deep,
Sometimes the ache of it is past my strength,
And yet for love of you I joy to weep,
My tears will fall beyond my lifetime's length.
Let me love you then — afar if needs must be —
Let me, as a tear, drop in your loving sea.

### 37

I love you, I love you, love you past sense;
I'm drunk, drunk, drunk with beauty, your beauty.
I'm dizzy, I'm giddy, stupid and dense,
Feckless, careless, forgetting my duty.
I live in a dream world where you are queen,
I wander, your clown, with my head in air;
I no longer know what half my words mean,
Let all the world fall, I no longer care.
Up, down, around, left, right, inside and out,
What does it matter, each second is bliss!
All laws and conventions I gladly flout,
Each person I meet I will gladly kiss.
Yet, fool that I am, who's more sane than I,
For not staying earthbound when I can fly?

### 38

One day you will come to me, that I know;
Some things are certain — as that day will dawn —
That rivers, widening, to the sea will flow —
That salmon swim against the stream to spawn.
But when that time will be I cannot tell,
No more than I can sure predict the tides;
That ringing day my hammer strikes your bell,
The Master Bellringer alone decides.
I do not pursue, do not make demand,
I love you, so your freedom I respect;
In His own time He'll wave the magic wand,
Of that new life He'll be the architect.
Meantime I will to work to love you more,
To scatter pearls to wash up on your shore.

### 39

In your presence I feel a great uplift,
A vast upsurge of spirit — marvellous!
This power you have is your unique gift,
Flows from you effortless, quite unconscious.
You are a catalyst to my dull will,
Inspiring, raising it to unknown height,
Your own will perfect, pure, unsullied, still;
A lambent candle lucent in my night.
I complicate, with my air and fire,
Verbose, loquacious, man of too much speech,
While you — clear water — earth — is your attire,
Your wordless waves wash straight up on the beach.
Apuleius worshipped Isis — wise man he!
Sea goddess, you are you, yet you are she.

### 40

I try to follow, dearest, your desire
To see you always just as fellow human;
Forget your gender, damp my manly fire,
Treat you as kindred spirit, not as woman.
When I succeed, see you as androgyne,
Myself the same, why then is Heaven there;
Then we're as angels, with no 'yours' and 'mine';
Then we're as one, a single fire and air.
But yesternight! Oh, yesternight! Your face
Across the table, chatting with our friends,
Its beauty! Oh, its beauty! My heart — race!
Quite overwhelmed — I'm lost — here my vow ends!
As man sees woman, that is how I saw;
Such beauty I could gaze on evermore.

## 41

I know a lovely river where Divine
And Holy Powers and Forces flow full spate,
And effortless turn water into wine,
And, brim with love, swift sweep away all hate.
This river is a gorgeous conduit,
An open channel with no hindrance there.
Fast flowing stream that will no rocks permit,
Such obstacles to love are soon worn bare.
Bathing in this river, I am reborn,
A child once more, I see the old world fresh;
Out there, on the horizon, breaks the dawn,
I'm for the open sea, freed from life's mesh.
Where is this river? Can you, dear, surmise?
I'll give you then the secret — in your eyes.


## 42

How can you know, how can you know, dear heart,
Oh, just how much, oh, just how much, how much
I love you — I would tear the world apart
For one brief gentle second of your touch.
A tender look from you can make my day,
Your smile makes candle of the brightest sun;
My step is lissom when you walk my way,
There is no other like you, none, none, none.
And yet if you denied me I'd not die,
And if you went away I would not pine,
I feel your love so vast it is my sky,
It's all around me, in me, has no line.
I love you, love you, love you — love, I burst;
Parched dry with life, you only slake my thirst.

### 43

It is enough I know you walk the earth;
It is enough — whether you're near or far,
I feel no loss, no emptiness, no dearth,
Where there is love, mere distance is no bar.
For my soul, your soul, they resonate in tune,
Each note from each complementing other
In pure harmonious orbit, sun and moon,
Gentle loving sister, loving brother,
We sing one song, whether I'm here, you're there,
Whether linked hand in hand, or worlds apart;
Sailing life's waters, turbulent with care,
We are one captain, with a single heart.
Below each other's horizon we may be,
No matter, for we sail the self-same sea.


### 44

When I am dead and gone, dear love, dead and gone,
My body wrapped in earth or ocean shroud;
When I am dead and gone, dear love, dead and gone,
My spirit soaring high above the cloud;
Then you will still be here upon the earth,
Living, loving, sailing the sun-kissed sea;
Your laughing, sparkling eyes still full of mirth;
Then tell me — will you ever think of me?
Perhaps, just now and then, dear love, now and then,
Your idling, wandering thought will on me dwell,
Remembering when I walked with living men,
Sad that my hammer did not strike your bell.
But I will still be here, dear love, still here;
Reading these lines once more, you'll feel me near.

## 45

Where you are there, the air is wholesome sweet,
All evil dark thoughts die as you walk by;
Where you are there, Divine and Human meet,
All clouds dissolve, revealing clear blue sky.
I love to tread the ground you've walked upon,
Breathe the self-same air you've lately breathed;
Each thing is holy where your glance has shone,
Radiant with the light by you bequeathed.
Around you is an aura of pure bliss,
Of bubbling joy, of love, of affirmation;
Negating thought of failure you dismiss,
Embracing gaily each new situation.
And yet you have your sadness, well I know,
A shadow with you everywhere you go.

## 46

I'm Love's sweet child! Spring flowers burst in joy!
The morning sun shines on my baby head;
I'm Love's sweet child! The whole world is my toy,
And I with Love's milk-honey feed am fed.
Your image in my heart forever glows,
Perpetual fuel for my ardent fire,
Your sparkling lovely waters feed my rose,
And petals I unfold of Love's Desire.
You do not know what worth you are to me,
You do not know you save my soul each day;
I'm stranded if I cannot sail your sea,
Bereft if I may never walk your way.
Mariner lost upon the ocean's night
Am I without your clear unclouded light.

## 47

I have no heart, I gave it all away;
I'm crucified, a scarecrow in the field;
I have no will, cannot say 'Yea' of 'Nay';
Can no longer fight, or no longer yield.
I'm nothing, flotsam, straw upon the wind,
Not even fly upon the window pane;
I cannot authorise, cannot rescind,
No longer balance book with 'Loss' or 'Gain'.
A feather blown about the void am I,
A no-thing, formless, lost in nothing — dead;
Yet, in spite of this, so alive am I,
I am a plenum — Cosmos is my bed.
Lost to myself, through my deep love for you,
I'm greater than I was — reborn — bright — new.

## 48

Men seek for gold among the wildest hills,
They seek it in fast-running mountain streams;
Men burrow underground with spades and drills,
Desperate to find that hidden vein that gleams.
They penetrate the deepest Arctic snows,
They hack their way through sunless forest's gloom;
The crack and rend apart vast iceberg floes,
The scour the desert, dive to ocean's womb.
For this lust for gold they kill each other,
Nothing stops or halts their maddened scrabble;
Hindered — thwarted — brother murders brother,
Ordered groups and crowds become a rabble.
To seek this gold, why tear the world apart?
I found it long ago — where? — in your heart.

## 49

Late spring — the wind is cold upon the sea
And cheek — East wind — treacherous and gusty;
Yet for the yacht, sailing westward, free.
But not for long — East's wind's never trusty,
We're bringing her home at last — she scents the way —
Rounding Land's end — the Longships — thoroughbred —
Pendeen abeam — course now hard to lay —
Put in a reef, for wind now from ahead.
Driving with engine and sail — now not far
To Hartland Point — a night of spray and foam —
Day dawns — we're in the Bay — across the Bar —
In smoother water now — moored up — we're home!
I briefly think of you — warmth floods my breast —
Give thanks — and then to blissful sleep and rest.

## 50

These my sonnets are 'As spells which unseal
Those inmost enchanted fountains of delight
Which is in the grief of love'. Spells which steal
Away the pain and drench me in Love's light.
Love is a many-petalled rose, and he
Who seeks to penetrate its inmost centre
Must prick his thumb upon that thorn called 'Me',
And lose himself 'fore he's allowed to enter.
Love is such pain, oh, such exquisite pain!
Let the thorn press deeper, ever deeper;
Deny Love not — it may not come again —
Let the path be steeper, ever steeper.
Yet so to ease the pain — oh, sonnets, glow!
Cast spells to make delighted fountains flow!

## 51

My heart is full — I find it hard to speak;
I think of you and tears are in my eyes.
I've found my love — no need to longer seek;
What have I done? Why should I win this prize?
And yet I have not won you — you are you —
Yourself —inviolate —mistress of your soul —
Although out giving, to yourself most true —
Complete and integrated, perfect whole.
Why should I want to win you, or possess?
Call you 'My own', say 'You belong to me'?
That is not love — no — that is selfishness;
There is no one to win you — you are free.
And that is why I love you — you are free;
Just as I love, yet do not own — the sea.


## 52

Let me be your knight and you my lady;
Let me wear your colours in my plume.
Vouchsafe this boon, chivalrous sweet lady,
I'll shine you light wherever shadows loom.
I'll slay you dragons, make your pathways straight,
Clear the dark wood, unbind you from all spells;
I'll banish ogres, open every gate,
All towers will peal for you their magic bells.
This our life is but a simple journey
From dark to light, from plain to mountain peak;
On the road many a tilt and tourney,
Where only Love can give you strength when weak.
A man, to be a man, needs be a knight,
And knight, sans lady, cannot scale the height.

## 53

Can I ever know the real you that is you,
Or is the you I know just in my mind?
How true or false is my rosy point of view?
Are you within and you without like kind?
I love you deeply, that I know for sure;
A hopeless love, exquisite pain, past sense;
But do I love my inner portraiture,
Or do I love your true real excellence?
I aim to love you, love you as you are,
Not my rosy-coloured wishful image;
Love each virtue, fault, each particular,
Love warm living being, not a mirage.
Yet I know, whatever image I adore,
The real you transcends, is so much more.


## 54

I seek myself, I ask myself, why, why
Do I forlorn so love you as I do?
Why do I love that laughter in your eye?
That sparkling eagerness for all things new?
You love me, that I know, yet in no sphere
More intimate than cherished life-long friend;
Although your face lights up when I appear,
Your love remains Platonic — there an end.
My love's comprehensive, all embracing,
Easily including Love Platonic —
The nearness of you — oh! — my heart's racing!
My condition's hopeless, cureless, chronic.
Why then do I love you? Oh, why ask why?
Tell me, why are we born? Why must we die?

## 55

Sometimes, alone in my monastic room,
And nodding quiet before an autumn fire,
My inward eye will gaze upon the loom
That weaves the tapestry on my life's gyre.
I see the cloth unroll upon the wheel,
Revealing threads of multi-varied cast,
Mosaic-ed life — artificial — real,
With good times, bad times, future, present, past,
And then, about two thirds along the way,
A different coloured thread comes into view;
A golden, gleaming, glistening, gilded ray,
Halo-ing my poor life — this thread is you.
Weaving iridescent, thread of pure delight,
Shining stream — from now my tapestry glows bright.


## 56

You are not here, you are not here, not here;
My world is empty, empty is my world.
Where are you? Where? You that I hold so dear?
While you're away, away, my ensign's furled.
There is a vacuum only you can 'phil',
Delicious pain you only can dispense;
Go away for ever, I'd love you still,
My Portsmouth Yardstick, you my excellence.
Each moment you're away I think of you,
Vicariously your pleasures I enjoy,
You may love me, leave me, be false or true,
But go adrift? — call me! — I'll be your buoy!
Until the flames leap up by your return,
My embered love will sure and steady burn.

## 57

The dial of my days has been put back,
And I grow ever younger hour by hour.
Though hove-to in Life's ocean, stopped in track,
Love's current sweeps me onward in full power.
I'm bald and what's left of my hair is white,
My skin, though clear, is wrinkled, freckled too,
And yet for me it's day, there is no night,
What was old when I was young is now so new,
I'm sailing ever forward to clear skies,
To new lands, leaving all that's old behind,
I'm sailing, dearest love, into your eyes,
Towards those Happy Isles I know I'll find,
I'll reach my Lyonesse, Elysium,
And bliss! Come over, I'll be overcome.


## 58

Let her go, I tell myself, let her go!
Forget her and forget her and forget.
She's but a flashing wave crest on Life's flow,
Golden gleam as the sun begins to set.
She is the moon strikes through the dolmen stone,
That instant streaks the old straight track ablaze,
A silver arch between the worlds she's thrown,
That weeps me up to heaven on its rays.
But then she's gone, and all is dark again,
I seldom see her, our roads drift apart,
So let her go, forget the pleasure, pain;
Redraw a new route on your ageing chart.
Fool! You cannot hold – let go – advance – retreat,
No more than you can cease your heart to beat!

## 59

When you smile, something happens to your face;
When you smile, something happens to your eyes.
A beam streaks down from heaven, leaves a trace
Of love, ocean-deep, Athene-wise.
A line forms round your mouth, lovely dimple,
Crinkly, enticing, totally unique;
Your face, round and moonlike, age-old, simple;
If anywhere, from there will heaven speak.
Why should mere lines around your eyes, your mouth,
Just by change of contour so enrapture?
At once, from north, I'm down in sunny south,
You, in smiling instant, my heart capture.
By your spellbinding magic, bold sea-maiden,
My soul's enchanted boat sails lightly laden.


## 60

Our chaste and snow white love has settled down,
We rest together in a tranquil sea.
In gentle sun-kissed waters do we drown,
Where, wordless, I am you and you are me.
What bliss it is to know and have such love,
So quiet and timeless, where no stress is there,
Where each is other's hand in other's glove,
Where each is other's joy, each other's care.
We do not need to meet each ev'ry day,
Mere space, time, and distance does not sever,
A thousand miles between — there's no 'away',
For us it's all before, now, and forever.
Our love lies like a lamb in our heart's core,
So pure and sweet we need desire no more.

www.ingramcontent.com/pod-product-compliance
Lightning Source LLC
Chambersburg PA
CBHW042127100526
44587CB00026B/4201